NAVIGATING THE
CYBERWORLD
WITH YOUR CHILD

NAVIGATING THE CYBERWORLD
WITH YOUR CHILD

A Guide for Parents, Teachers and Counsellors

Edited by Dr Ong Say How
and Tan Yi Ren

Marshall Cavendish
Editions

Cover image credit: Tinxi/ Shutterstock.com
Design: Benson Tan

Published by Marshall Cavendish Editions
An imprint of Marshall Cavendish International
1 New Industrial Road, Singapore 536196

Other Marshall Cavendish Offices:
Marshall Cavendish Corporation. 99 White Plains Road, Tarrytown NY 10591-9001, USA • Marshall Cavendish International (Thailand) Co Ltd. 253 Asoke, 12th Flr, Sukhumvit 21 Road, Klongtoey Nua, Wattana, Bangkok 10110, Thailand • Marshall Cavendish (Malaysia) Sdn Bhd, Times Subang, Lot 46, Subang Hi-Tech Industrial Park, Batu Tiga, 40000 Shah Alam, Selangor Darul Ehsan, Malaysia.

Marshall Cavendish is a trademark of Times Publishing Limited

National Library Board, Singapore Cataloguing-in-Publication Data
Name(s): Ong, Say How, editor. | Tan, Yi Ren, editor.
Title: Navigating the cyberworld with your child : a guide for parents, teachers and counsellors / edited by Ong Say How and Tan Yi Ren.
Description: Singapore : Marshall Cavendish Editions,[2016]
Identifier(s): OCN 945900258 | ISBN 978-981-47-2197-4 (paperback)
Subject(s): LCSH: Internet addiction in adolescence. | Internet addiction in adolescence--Prevention. | Internet and children. | Internet and youth.
Classification: DDC 616.858400835--dc23

Printed in Singapore by JCS Digital Solutions Pte Ltd

CONTENTS

PREFACE

The arrival of the Internet in the late 1980s marks the beginning of the golden age in information communication and technology. The Internet opens up the whole world and in a way brings people closer together across cultures, zones and boundaries.

Singapore, like many countries with high economic growth and population density, is ranked one of the top three Asian countries with a high proportion of its population accessing and using the Internet. As of January 2015, Singapore has the highest download broadband speed in the world (Ookla, 2015), with 80% of its 5.5 million people using the Internet (Internet Live stats, 2014). Most of the users fall within the 25-34 year old age group with the 15-24 year olds coming in at a close second. In terms of mobile connectivity, Singapore has a mobile penetration rate of 152%, with about 8.3 million active mobile subscriptions (We Are Social, 2015). The frightening fact is that Singaporeans have about 3.3

connected devices each, with smartphones being the most used device!

Fuelled by a huge customer demand created by social and print media, advertisements and peer influences, the Internet is now increasingly considered a basic necessity of Generation Z. Nevertheless, like most inventions, there are downsides and Internet addiction is a real problem. With it, related behaviours like Internet shopping, gaming and gambling addictions have become societal issues that cannot be completely ignored.

As a mental health professional, it is increasingly common to see a young person being brought to the clinic or hospital by their parents or caregivers for compulsive or unhealthy use of the computer and the Internet. Whether Internet addiction is considered a clinical disorder is very much still debatable but we know that its severity is highly correlated with that of comorbid psychiatric disorders. Preliminary local research suggests high levels of anxiety and depressive symptoms among those inflicted with Internet addiction, and a possibility of them (Internet addiction and psychiatric conditions) mutually reinforcing each other.

I hope this book will be able to inform readers about Internet use, its possible problems and how to go about getting help if they observe a young person who is using the Internet in a compulsive or pathological manner. Individuals who are at risk can seek help from several professional services in Singapore, such as the National Addictions Management Service (NAMS) in the Institute of Mental Health and TOUCH Cyber Wellness (see pg 169 for a list of resources). As many individuals suffering from Internet addiction and related behaviours are youths and young persons, this book is specifically targeted at parents, teachers and counsellors.

Dr Ong Say How
Senior Consultant Psychiatrist
Child Guidance Clinic
Institute of Mental Health

WHAT IS ADDICTION?

Dr Ong Say How

WHAT IS ADDICTION?

Addiction has been defined as "compulsive behaviors that persist despite serious negative consequences for personal, social, or occupational function" (Camí & Farré, 2003). It is a condition characterised by the compulsive and continued use of a substance or drug (e.g., alcohol, heroin, amphetamine, nicotine) or engagement in an activity (e.g., gambling, shopping, watching pornography) to such an extent that it interferes with the social, academic and occupational functioning of the individual.

Addiction can be experienced either physically or psychologically. Physical addiction describes a biological state in which the body needs a higher and higher dosage of a drug in order to achieve its intended pleasurable or euphoric effect. This is called tolerance. The drug intake or involvement in addictive behaviour must be both psychologically reinforcing (increases the likelihood of further repeated use) and intrinsically rewarding (perception as being positive or desirable). Individuals who are addicted typically lack awareness and insight that their behaviour is out of control and causing problems to themselves and others.

Dependence describes an adaptive state associated with a withdrawal syndrome upon cessation of repeated exposure to a stimulus (drug or activity). The individual suffers withdrawal during which the body reacts adversely to the cessation of the drug, causing physical-somatic (e.g., nausea, diarrhoea, bodily pains, tremors, fatigue, sweating, confusion) and emotional-motivational withdrawal symptoms (e.g., depression, anxiety, frustration, feeling unease, intense craving, mood irritability and reduced capacity to experience pleasure). Dependence continues because the withdrawal effects are so unpleasant that the individual has to rapidly resume taking the drug or the behaviour to relieve those symptoms.

In summary, addiction is a compulsion for rewarding stimuli that is mediated through positive reinforcement while dependence, which is mediated through negative reinforcement, involves a desire to use a drug or perform a behaviour to avoid the unpleasant withdrawal symptoms that results from cessation of exposure to it.

Many have debated whether addiction is a "disease", a "social problem" or a true mental illness, and whether drug dependence and addiction mean the same thing. Even medical experts do not always agree on this.

The underlying mechanism for addiction lies primarily in the reward circuitry system in the brain. When consumed, a psychoactive drug mimics the effect of the brain's key neurotransmitter, dopamine, which is involved in the experience of pleasure. Other neurotransmitters such as glutamate and serotonin, however, work through other mechanisms to reinforce the reward system through the learning and remembering of a reward experience and emotional regulation of reward-seeking behaviour respectively. After prolonged usage, the brain adapts by down-regulating the number of receptors for dopamine or produce less natural dopamine, thus reducing the ability to experience pleasure. Therefore, the addict has to take an ever-increasing amount of the drug to achieve its intended "high" effect.

Because psychoactive drugs are extremely potent in causing the release of dopamine (up to ten times more than natural rewards), an addict soon chooses to use these drugs rather than rely on naturally rewarding behaviours.

EARLY RESEARCH AND CLASSIFICATION OF ADDICTION

Early research in addictions delved largely on alcohol abuse and dependence. The early definition of alcohol dependence was based on work done in 1976, when the British psychiatrist Griffith Edwards and his American colleague Milton M. Gross collaborated to produce a formulation of what had previously been understood as alcoholism – the alcohol dependence syndrome. The Edwards & Gross criteria consists of the following elements for which the degree of dependence is judged:

- Narrowing of the drinking repertoire
- Increased salience of the need for alcohol over competing needs and responsibilities

- An acquired tolerance to alcohol
- Withdrawal symptoms
- Relief or avoidance of withdrawal symptoms by further drinking
- Subjective awareness of compulsion to drink
- Reinstatement after abstinence

In the latest edition of the *Diagnostic and Statistical Manual of Mental Disorders* (DSM-5), published by the American Psychiatric Association and used to help clinicians and researchers diagnose and classify mental disorders, addiction is categorised under substance-related and addictive disorders.

In DSM-5, substance-related disorders have been sub-grouped into alcohol, caffeine, hallucinogen, cannabis, cocaine, sedative/hypnotic/anxiolytic, stimulant, solvent inhalant and tobacco-related. Gambling disorder remains the only non-substance-related disorder (behavioural addiction) described in DSM-5, as evidenced by similar activation of the reward systems as drugs of abuse. Other forms of behavioural addictions, e.g., using the Internet, sex, shopping, exercise etc., have not been included due to insufficient scientific evidence and a lack of consensus in establishing diagnostic criteria.

Addiction is very different from a habit. All of us have habits or rituals of some sort that we carry out in our daily lives. Habits are done by choice and one can decide when to stop. However, a habit can eventually develop into an addiction. What started out innocently as an enjoyable activity without any significant problems soon takes on a life of its own and we cannot stop carrying out that habit, invariably leading to psychological and/or physical negative effects.

Whether physical or psychological in nature, the individual is unable to control the aspects of the addiction alone or without help from medical professionals and their loved ones.

COMMON FEATURES AMONG ADDICTIONS

When a person is addicted to a substance, they lack the ability to control its use and would continue taking it at the expense of their health, even if it is causing harm to themselves or others. Substance dependence can cause powerful cravings, which the person finds very hard to overcome.

- The person engages in taking the substance or in the activity repeatedly and cannot stop despite multiple prior attempts.

- An addict has to take an increasing amount of the drug or do more of the activity in order to achieve its intended effect.

- Presence of withdrawal symptoms and cravings – when the substance gradually disappears from the body or upon cessation of the activity, the addict experiences physical and mood-related symptoms.

- Taking unnecessary and impulsive risks – done in the process of obtaining the drug or engaging in the activity despite knowing its risks and dangers, e.g., breaking the law.

- Substance use or activity involvement becomes an obsession and compulsion – the mind is preoccupied with means and ways to obtain the drug or engage in the activity.

- Substance use or activity as a means to cope with problems – e.g., an alcoholic drinking to forget about his marital woes, a game addict immerses himself in "alternate-world" computer games to avoid real-life problems.
- Secrecy and solitude – addicted individuals usually take their substance or partake in their activities alone to avoid detection by family members.
- Denial – a hallmark of addiction is that addicted individuals refuse to acknowledge or are simply not aware that they have a problem.
- At the expense of one's physical health – e.g., an alcoholic with liver cirrhosis still continues drinking hard liquor. An Internet addict may omit food and drinks to continue his pursuits online.
- At the expense of social and family relationships – social/recreational activities as well as important family gatherings and events are often given up in order to use the drug or engage in the activity.
- Financial difficulties – at some point, the substance use or activity demands huge expenditures and time away from work or studies. Borrowing or stealing of money from family members and others can happen. The addict is also likely to lose his job due to frequent absenteeism and deterioration in work quality, leading to financial woes.
- Run-ins with the law – typically in relation to drug intoxication or impulsivity as a result of disinhibitory effects caused by drugs. Also, the addict might commit crimes to get money to pay for his addiction. Domestic

and spousal violence, separation and divorce are very common as well. Legal problems could also arise in Internet and Internet-related addictions (addressed in Chapter Seven).

CAUSES OF ADDICTION

As with most social issues and mental illnesses, the causes of addiction are multifactorial, of which many are still not well understood. It would therefore be correct to say that there is generally a combination of social, physical, psychological, emotional and circumstantial factors and it is the interplay of all these factors that contributes to the development of addiction.

In general, males between 18 to 35 years of age are more likely to engage in addictive behaviours. While addiction was associated with poverty, ghettos and gangs in the past, it has been increasingly apparent that social class differences are no longer as strong a factor in predicting addiction. Many young people, ranging from middle-income households to those from well-to-do families, are experimenting with synthetic drugs or using them recreationally. The following are certain factors that may increase the risk:

- Nature (Genetics) – It has been estimated that 40-60% of the vulnerability to developing an addiction is due to genetics. In a Swedish study on 18,000 adopted children, adopted children whose biological parents abused drugs were found to be twice as likely to do so themselves, compared with adopted children whose birth parents did not abuse drugs. Adopted children also had about twice the risk of drug abuse if either their biological full or half-sibling had a drug abuse problem. In addition, genes responsible for mental illnesses could themselves make a person more vulnerable to developing substance abuse.

- Nurture (Environment) – People with parents who are drug addicts or are living with a close relative with an addiction problem have a higher risk of eventually becoming one themselves. Growing up in a drug-taking environment surrounded by drugs and drug paraphernalia or witnessing parents taking drugs, not only desensitises a young person to drugs, but also makes the drugs easily available.

- Mental condition – People with chronic anxiety, depression, Attention Deficit Hyperactivity Disorder (ADHD) and specific types of personality disorders (that involve high novelty-seeking, low harm avoidance, low reward dependence) with tendencies for risk-taking, impulsiveness and behavioural undercontrol, have a higher risk of eventually becoming addicted to drugs, alcohol or nicotine.

- Peer pressure and loneliness – Young people can be pressured to do things they do not wish to do, including smoking and drug-taking. The pressure to conform and to gain acceptance is particularly strong for young people. Young people also tend to feel easily bored or lonely. Taking drugs together can provide that connection with peers.

- Family attachment – Young people who do not have a strong attachment to their families or grow up in an invalidating, critical or hostile home environment are more at risk. Abuse (whether neglect, physical or sexual) also predisposes a person to drug abuse. In some cases, individuals take drugs to escape from their harsh realities or to cope with past trauma.

NEW ONSET OF BEHAVIOURAL ADDICTIONS

With the advances in info-technology and the human's perpetual need to seek novel sensations, new addictive behaviours have emerged and are now being studied. To date, much is still unknown about them. More research studies are beginning to offer deeper insight into the understanding of behavioural addictions and there is an increasing number of data published on the topics of the Internet and Internet-related addictions. Without a doubt, unless we recognise the addiction symptoms and intervene early, more social, physical and mental health problems are likely to arise.

The topic of new behavioural addictions will be covered in the following chapters.

ADDICTION AND THE INTERNET

Dr Gomathinayagam Kandasami
Dr Mythily Subramaniam

INTERNET ADDICTION: DEFINITION AND HISTORY

The Internet is a part of most people's lives today, with research suggesting that approximately 40% of the world's population is online. People use the Internet to gather and disseminate information, gain knowledge, maintain relationships, and even make money. Compared to 2000, the USA has more than doubled its usage in 2011 (Nielsen, 2012), indicating that Internet use has become a highly prevalent activity for both adolescents and adults. Local data from Singapore suggests that in 2013, 81% of the population had used the Internet at least once in the past 12 months as compared to 2003, when only 53% endorsed past year use (IDA, 2013).

Building on Chapter One's description of addiction, Internet addiction refers to the excessive and uncontrolled use of the Internet which interferes with a person's daily life. In other words, it is a maladaptive pattern of Internet use, generally time-consuming, that leads to significant impairment or distress. In this chapter and throughout the book, Internet use refers to accessing the Internet via various Internet-enabled devices, such as computers, laptops, smartphones and tablets. A number of other terms have been used for this condition such as problematic Internet use, compulsive Internet use, pathological Internet use, excessive Internet use or iDisorder. However, it would seem still very early to use a single umbrella term or label to define the nature of Internet-related problems as many studies conducted in this field so far have presented varying degrees of differences with mixed results.

Internet addiction was first researched by Dr Kimberly Young who presented her findings on over 600 cases of Internet users at the American Psychological Association annual meeting in 1996. She used an adapted version of the criteria for pathological gambling in the *Diagnostic and Statistical Manual of Mental Disorders* (DSM-IV) to classify the users. Respondents who answered "yes" to five or more of the criteria were classified as addicted Internet users (dependents) and the remainder were classified as normal Internet users (non-dependents) for the purposes of the study. Since the criteria were derived from those for pathological gambling, which at the time was classified as an impulse control disorder, she suggested that addicted Internet users had an impulse control disability which needed further investigation.

WHAT IS INTERNET ADDICTION?

To date there is no consensus on whether Internet addiction is a separate mental disorder, a manifestation of underlying mental disorders or, whether it is a disorder at all. Ha and colleagues (2006) summarised that Internet addiction is considered by various researchers as "a genuine diagnosis, a new symptom manifestation of underlying disorders; or psychosocial problems in adjusting to a new medium".

Some researchers consider Internet addiction to be a part of impulse control disorder, which is defined as the failure to resist an impulsive act or behaviour that may be harmful to self or others. These behaviours are not premeditated and the person has little or no control over the behaviour. Acting on these "impulses" causes pleasure or gratification which is similar to the feelings experienced among people with Internet addiction who are unable to resist the "urge" to spend long hours on the Internet and giving in to the urge provides them with pleasure.

Others have suggested that it is a behavioural addiction. Similar to many substance use disorders, the person with Internet addiction experiences "preoccupation" with the Internet, withdrawal symptoms (feelings of anger, irritation and low moods) when the Internet is not available, tolerance (the need to spend more and more time on the Internet to achieve the same "high"), loss of other interests, unsuccessful attempts to quit, and use of the Internet to improve or escape dysphoric mood (APA, 2013). The person continues with the behaviour despite adverse consequences such as fights with other family members, poor performance at work or school and social isolation.

It has also been observed that a number of mental disorders co-occur with Internet addiction. This has led to debates as to whether Internet addiction is the cause or consequence of these associated mental disorders. Some researchers suggest that excessive use of the Internet is a secondary manifestation of depression, anxiety or other mental disorders or a form of escape from existing mental states and may represent adaptive "self-soothing".

DIAGNOSIS OF INTERNET ADDICTION

A large number of assessment tools in different languages are available to assess Internet addiction. Why the large number? This is because different researchers have their own interpretation or thoughts of the problem and there are no established diagnostic criteria for Internet addiction as yet. The three most frequently used questionnaires are detailed below:

INTERNET ADDICTION TEST

IAT (Young, 1998), is composed of 20 items and is scored on a 6-point scale. The cut-off scores proposed for the 6-point scale IAT classify Internet users as those with "No Impairment"(0-30), "Mild" (31–49), "Moderate" (50–79) and "Severe" impairment (80–100). Examples of the questions include:

- How often do you find that you stay online longer than you intended?
- How often do you feel depressed, moody or nervous when you are offline, which goes away once you are back online?

COMPULSIVE INTERNET USE SCALE

CIUS (Meerkerk et al., 2009) includes 14 items on a 5-point Likert scale. It has also been validated in a 9-item form for adolescents. Cut-off scores of 21 have been suggested as appropriate for prevalence estimation of problematic Internet use. Examples of questions include:

- How often do you find it difficult to stop using the Internet when you are online?
- How often do others (e.g., partner, children, parents, friends) say you should use the Internet less?

CHEN INTERNET ADDICTION SCALE

CIAS (Chen et al., 2003) comprises 26 items and is scored on a 4-point Likert scale. A cut-off of 57/ 58 has been suggested for screening and 63/64 for diagnosis. This scale has been widely used in Chinese populations.

THEORIES AND CAUSES OF INTERNET ADDICTION

Despite the lack of universal agreement on the specific diagnostic criteria for Internet addiction, people do genuinely struggle with life and emotional difficulties such as stress, depression, anxiety, job burnout, academic troubles, sudden unemployment and marital discord because of their excessive Internet use. It is therefore important for professionals and the public to understand the causative factors as better understanding of the underlying mechanisms can help achieve positive treatment outcomes. Various theories have been put forth by experts in this area to understand what makes someone addicted to the Internet.

DESCRIPTIVE MODELS

Some experts have proposed a four-factor model to describe problematic Internet use.

- Factor one mainly focuses on the various dysfunctional Internet behaviours associated with its overuse.
- Factor two describes the normal functional use of the Internet in a productive and meaningful way.
- Factor three focuses on using the Internet for sexual gratification and/or social gains. This describes how a shy or introverted user would rely on the Internet to express his/her fantasies.
- Factor four describes a disinterested behaviour towards the Internet and thereby demonstrating little or no risk of developing Internet addiction.

Critics argue that whilst this model is helpful in describing the category of Internet usage on any given user, it does not address the underlying mechanisms behind addictive and dysfunctional Internet behaviour.

GROHOL'S PHASES MODEL OF PATHOLOGICAL INTERNET USE

Grohol (1999) suggested that Internet behaviour falls into three phases. In Stage One, the user who is a newcomer is first exposed to the Internet and acclimatises to this new technology by immersing himself in it. This phase of "enchantment" with this technology results in an overuse of the technology. In Stage Two, the online user becomes disillusioned or even bored with the new technology and begins to avoid using the technology. The user finally moves into Stage Three, where he finds a balance and begins to use the new technology at a "normal" level and responsibly integrates the Internet into his life. The model assumes that all online activity is phasic to some degree and that all people will eventually get to Stage Three on their own. While some may get stuck in Stage One for a longer time, they will progress to Stage Three though it may take them longer than others.

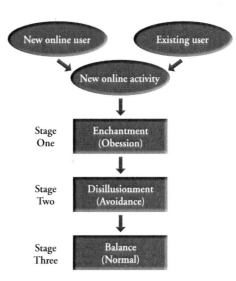

THREE As ENGINE MODEL

The three As – Anonymity, Accessibility and Affordability – offered by the Internet also make users vulnerable to addictive behaviour. The anonymity of the Internet encourages users to feel more open and frank in talking with other users. It helps users feel comfortable without being judged by others. The privacy of the Internet enables intimacy that may increase the risk of a cyber affair. Easy accessibility and affordability of several interactive online applications such as WhatsApp and Facebook can make communication and meeting with others a lot easier. A simple innocent post or an email exchange can quickly lead and escalate into an intense cyber affair of a sexual nature. It is hypothesised that the "high" or emotional escape provided by interactive Internet activity coupled with the enabling influence of the three As reinforce and condition the mind positively, resulting in increased compulsivity.

INTERNET ADDICTION – GENERALISED AND SPECIFIC TYPES

Addiction to Internet use can be seen as either generalised or specific. The generalised type is conceptualised as multidimensional. It involves spending large amounts of time on the Internet with no directive purpose, for example, spending time endlessly in chat rooms or surfing the Internet. People with generalised addiction problems face more personal and professional consequences that are unlikely to have happened in the absence of the Internet. Research shows these people to be more prone to suffering from pre-existing psychological difficulties. They may be experiencing negative perceptions about themselves or about the world; self-doubt or be prone to maladaptive ruminative thoughts and behaviours related to Internet use; or be socially isolated.

They may also use the Internet without any directive purpose and hence waste a lot of time. Virtual, rather than face-to-face, communication acts as their main source of contact to the outside world. They face huge problems with their daily functioning due to their desire to sustain a virtual, social life. Hence they tend to procrastinate on tasks that they need to engage in and subsequently experience high stress levels over time. This vicious cycle of inactivity followed by emotional difficulties contributes to both the development and maintenance of their addictive online behaviour.

The specific type of Internet addiction, on the other hand, is very much content related. Particularly, this affects those who have already been struggling with a pre-existing addiction problem offline. An example would be an offline compulsive gambler who decides to go online because of the availability of gambling online. Subsequently he/she faces more problems with online gambling-related Internet activity. Another example would be someone with compulsive sexual behaviour crossing into problematic online sexual behaviour because of the easy access to and availability of pornographic material online.

CAUSATIVE FACTORS OF INTERNET ADDICTION

PSYCHOLOGICAL FACTORS

The cognitive-behavioural model (Davis, 2001) suggests that one of the components for development of problematic Internet use is the presence of maladaptive thinking related to irrational beliefs. Maladaptive thoughts usually refer to one's problematic self-perception and world view. People with a tendency to self-doubt, experience low self-worth, self-blame and self-deprecate may view the Internet as a non-threatening medium to receive positive responses about themselves. For example, these people may see the Internet as the only place that they can feel good in and often feel more empowered there than when offline. They may see the Internet as the only friendly and safe place in their life. They may also believe that nobody loves them in real life compared to how they are perceived online. Excessive generalisations and "all-or-nothing" types of thought patterns leading to thoughts such as "I am good only on the Internet" and "I am a failure when I am not on the Internet" (Davis, 2001) result in the worsening of problematic Internet use. These distorted thoughts can be automatically triggered during chatting or networking which in turn positively reinforce and condition the mind to maintain repetitive compulsive online behaviour.

Internet and associated technologies also increase the vulnerability to addiction by positively reinforcing the same behaviour. When a person initially tries a new Internet feature, the chances of doing it again are determined by the type of response received. If the response is positive, then it encourages the user to continue with that activity. Some examples are getting a "like" or receiving a positive comment for posting a picture on Facebook. The person is then conditioned to perform that activity more often to achieve the same positive response as the one associated with the initial event. This conditioning of response continues until the person eventually tries to explore other novel technologies to achieve a similar positive physical and psychological reaction and therefore increases the risk for addictive Internet use.

In the context of Internet use, any stimuli such as seeing a smartphone being used by someone or hearing a "ping" sound of a notification message on another person's smartphone can easily trigger a conditioned Internet-based response. This phenomenon is commonly termed secondary reinforcement. These situational cues can reinforce the development of compulsive Internet use and contribute to the maintenance of associated symptoms.

People who have a tendency to ruminate about themselves can also become vulnerable to more severe and prolonged problems with Internet use. Ruminative styles may vary. Some may end up talking to friends while others may try to read vigorously to find out more about their excessive use of the Internet. These people may keep worrying and thinking about their Internet use instead of trying to find a solution to reduce their activity. This ruminative style of thinking increases the chances of recalling more positive memories of using the Internet and therefore enabling the user to maintain the same level of Internet activity that they struggle to control. These people also stop taking corrective actions or engaging with others to solve their problems.

BIOLOGICAL FACTORS

Very few studies have explored the brain mechanisms underpinning the addictive properties of the Internet. Internet addiction has not been included as a diagnosis in the recently revised DSM-5 classification system mainly because of the dearth of supportive neurobiological evidence. Nevertheless, results from a few neuroimaging studies suggest that the craving in online gaming addiction and craving seen in substance dependence may share the same neurobiological mechanisms. Some studies reported degenerative changes in the brain's grey matter, reduced functional connectivity between the brain cells and reduced thickening of brain cortex, but it is still not clear from existing research as to whether these findings are directly linked to Internet-related addictive behaviours.

There is also some evidence that genetic factors may play a role in the development of Internet addiction. A study from South Korea showed association between Internet addiction and abnormalities in genes influencing certain personality traits such as harm avoidance, characterised by excessive worrying and pessimism and novelty-seeking, characterised by tendencies to seek thrills, be impulsive, avoid frustration and lose one's temper easily.

A few studies also report similar brain mechanisms for the compulsive behaviour seen in Obsessive-Compulsive Disorder (OCD) and Internet addiction.

COMPENSATION THEORY

Both adults and adolescents can use the Internet as a means to compensate for their psychosocial problems that arise due to poor self-esteem, self-identity, and difficulties in interpersonal communication. This is well supported by research findings showing higher levels of loneliness among students who were considered to be pathological or addicted users of the Internet. It has been shown that cyberspace helps those who feel awkward in social situations to connect with others in a non-threatening way. It provides a supportive medium that enables them to express themselves more freely online, as well as to experience the warmth, friendship and acceptance that are missing in their real lives. They may thus compensate for their difficulties and shortcomings by hiding behind the secrecy of the Internet despite facing negative outcomes due to their compulsive use.

PERSONALITY FACTORS

Studies reveal that adolescents who display structured behaviour may run a lower risk of Internet addiction compared to those who are disorganised. People with a tendency to readily experience anger, anxiety, irritability, apprehension, depression, and feelings of insecurity have also been shown to be associated with high rates of problematic Internet use. Adolescents who are less extroverted and more open to experience are likely to use the Internet more frequently and they may be at a higher risk of developing Internet addiction. However, these findings should be interpreted with caution due to the small number of participants and biased clinical samples reported in the studies.

SITUATIONAL FACTORS

Problematic Internet behaviours can be triggered by situational factors too. People who experience stressful life events can use the Internet momentarily to escape from their real life situations. Online networking through friends or playing a game or watching porn can all help to fill up the void created by the stressful situations. However, using the Internet for a momentary escape from situational stress may not necessarily make someone addicted to it instantaneously. It is true that many can stop their online behaviour over a period of time. However, the risk increases the moment people tend to persist with their online activities as the only mechanism to cope with their situation. As the behaviour escalates, it can become very compulsive and unmanageable. People can jeopardise their careers and relationships. Dissatisfaction in life, missing close intimate relationships and feeling hopeless about a life situation are some of the risk factors associated with Internet addiction.

SOCIO-ECONOMIC FACTORS

Internet addiction is predominantly associated with the male gender. Particularly, males tend to show more online gaming- and cybersex-related addiction problems. Internet addiction is also prevalent among adolescents with higher family income status, being a senior in high school and low academic achievement. Furthermore, the risk seems to be also high among adolescents who experience family conflicts and inconsistent parental supervision of their Internet use. However, one should bear in mind that these socioeconomic risks may not have any direct causal relationship with Internet addiction.

RELATIONSHIP BETWEEN INTERNET ADDICTION AND MENTAL HEALTH DISORDERS

People with Internet addiction were reported to experience high rates of depressive symptoms. But it is not clear whether the presence of depressive symptoms is a cause or effect. Nevertheless, studies have shown that Internet addiction and clinical depressive symptoms are highly correlated and they reinforce one another. It is hypothesised that people who are depressed are more likely to use the Internet to cope with their negative emotions due to their underlying fear of rejection, low motivation and self-esteem difficulties.

People who are already struggling with substance addiction problems are also vulnerable to Internet addiction. It is hypothesised that these people who have been trying to cope with their existing difficulties surrounding addictive substance may shift their coping strategy towards the Internet because they may see the latter as a convenient, legal, and physically safe distraction compared to their drug of choice. They may also believe that being addicted to the Internet is medically safer than being addicted to drugs or alcohol. Similarly, people with sex addiction problems can find a new source of sexual gratification through watching pornography online. By providing a new, seemingly anonymous and socially acceptable way of coping, the Internet enables them to continue with their excessive sexual behaviours without the physical need of visiting commercial sex workers.

Some studies also point out a high prevalence of bipolar affective disorder (a mood disorder characterised by extreme mood swings) among problematic Internet users. Anxiety disorders, psychotic disorders, personality disorders (borderline, narcissistic and antisocial types) and Attention Deficit Hyperactive Disorder (ADHD) are some of the other mental disorders associated with Internet addiction. There is also a correlation among the frequency of Internet use, past mental health treatments and suicidal intent. However, caution is required when interpreting these findings in view of the small numbers and inherent biases that were reported in the studies.

IMPLICATIONS

There are no easy answers in the debate regarding the existence of Internet addiction. While methodological problems remain, preliminary studies which have been conducted so far in this field give us a good general understanding of how vulnerable people interact with the Internet and how their interactions can progress into a trajectory of addiction. Data especially from Asian countries suggests that problematic or addictive Internet behaviour does exist and the psychosocial and relationship problems caused are comparable with those caused by other, more established forms of addiction.

However, many who use the Internet may not end up using it excessively or find it hard to control their behaviour. Maladaptive core personal beliefs, thoughts and behaviours play a major role in both the development and maintenance of problematic or addictive Internet behaviour. People with low self-esteem and negative self-appraisal run a high risk of developing Internet addiction because they may use the Internet as an escape mechanism to avoid real or perceived problems in their lives. They may be encouraged by the anonymous, non-inhibiting and non-face-to-face communication offered by the Internet in order to overcome their perceived inadequacies. This can eventually lead to addiction. Mental health disorders such as depression, anxiety and bipolar affective disorder may also increase the risks.

We may see more cases of Internet addiction in the future due to vast advances made in Internet technologies. Therefore, to pursue with effective treatment programmes, continued research is needed to better understand this phenomenon. Assessment criteria need to be validated with clinical diagnosis, interventions need to be evaluated rigorously and more research needs to be done using longitudinal studies to understand the underlying biology and natural course of the disorder. Specifically, future research should target more on how mental health problems, personality traits, family dynamics, and interpersonal skills, all influence the way people utilise the Internet.

INTERNET ADDICTION IN THE YOUNG

Dr Ong Say How
Tan Yi Ren

CASE STUDY

Fabian Tan is 15 and attends a mainstream secondary school. He lives with his parents and two older siblings. Both his parents are working. The Tans are a typical upper middle class family, living in a five-room flat in a relatively young housing estate.

Fabian has a history of being hyperactive as a child and is generally weaker in his studies compared to his two older siblings. Despite tuition and enrichment classes, he struggled in his studies. He was reluctant to do his homework and revisions, and would bargain for more time on his computer or PlayStation in primary school. In Primary Five, he began using the computer at home without much adult supervision as both his parents were working and his domestic helper was no longer able to get him to comply with her requests like before. When his parents got home late at night, he was already too tired and had gone off to bed. As he reached Primary Six, he was just getting by academically and his teachers had given up "chasing" him for schoolwork and complaining about him to his parents.

In the early secondary years, Fabian talked about quitting school with his friends. He felt that what he learnt in school was boring and not relevant to him. He had, however, no plans for himself in the future, like what his ambition was or what courses he would like to study in higher institutions. Slowly over the years, Fabian got increasingly restless in class and started to skip lessons whenever he had the chance to. He would stay at home and play on his computer, mostly enjoying his online games and surfing the Internet aimlessly, depending on what got his attention that day. He watched YouTube videos endlessly ever since there was an explosion of people posting their homemade videos online. While his school attendance dwindled, he ceased going out with his family members for outings or meals. He cited numerous excuses or simply ignored his parents' requests. As Fabian had a bedroom to himself, he locked his bedroom door and his parents were unable to gain access to him or stop him in his online games.

As Fabian's school attendance worsened to the point of him missing his class tests, his parents panicked and unlocked his room using the spare key. They attempted to remove his computer but this was met with huge resistance from Fabian. The struggle escalated into a violent episode during which Fabian hit his father and broke his glasses. His parents had to vacate his room because they were worried for their own safety. They had also tried terminating his online account but Fabian would throw a huge temper tantrum until his parents relented. At other times, he would go out to the neighbourhood LANS shop or Internet cafe to continue his gaming or Internet surfing. Over time, Fabian stopped going to school completely, and was not receptive to the school's multiple attempts to engage him back to school. He spent nearly twelve hours on the computer, and neglected his personal self-care and grooming as he did not see a need to perform them. He rationalised that he would be at home all the time anyway. He also had irregular meals and would rather rampage through his home fridge for leftover food than go to the nearby hawker centre to purchase his meals. Soon, he started to smell since he hardly changed his clothes and his room was in a mess. There was no longer a differentiation of day and night. He would sleep in the daytime and be awake at night so that he could join other international players in the online games. If he were to miss a session on the computer, he would feel easily agitated, angry and restless. These would typically be relieved by a return to his online games or YouTube videos.

APPEAL OF THE INTERNET

The use of the Internet has increased greatly in recent years. Its explosive growth over the past decades has reshaped the way we communicate and seach for information. Many traditional modes of media and entertainment are now found online. New communication tools have also been developed so that people can chat, share information and interact with each other in this virtual world. These tools include, but are not limited to, instant messaging platforms, forums and social networking sites. The Internet has introduced convenience to people's lives, but it presents both opportunities as well as risks if not used wisely.

Before we begin to understand Internet addiction, it would be good to look into some features of the Internet. In general, many functions on the Internet are stimulating and user-friendly. A single click or swipe on the devices can provide immediate and rapid responses. This allows users to be instantly rewarded and hence behaviours on the Internet are positively reinforced. Furthermore, many Internet users like the feature of perceived anonymity, in which they are able to surf the Internet without disclosing their own identity. In individual profiles on social networking sites, they can also choose to portray the positive and favourable characteristics of themselves.

The next feature of the Internet is the ability to stay connected with others online. The Internet allows people worldwide to connect with each other and establish interpersonal relationships regardless of the boundaries of time and physical location. The communication mode in the past, which may take days or weeks, can be done almost instantly now. Photo sharing, status updating and interacting with one another on social networking sites are crucial in maintaining relationships online. Online gaming applications also incorporate functions which allow gamers to communicate with each other while playing games. All these features are particularly attractive for many Internet users. However, they also introduce some new problems in our modern society, one of which is Internet addiction.

INTERNET ADDICTION

What is Internet addiction? As explained in Chapter Two, it is characterised by the excessive use of various Internet-enabled devices which results in significant impairment in daily lives. These include failures in school or at work, disruptions to daily routines, as well as interpersonal relationship issues with family members and other individuals. This chapter will focus on the generalised type of Internet addiction, which involves spending excessive amounts of time on the Internet with no direct purpose. Specific types of Internet addiction (e.g., social media, online gaming, online gambling) will be covered in the subsequent chapters.

Some researchers explore and compare Internet addiction with substance use disorder. Both addictions are similar in some ways. For instance, those who are addicted to either the Internet or substance use often display withdrawal and tolerance symptoms. They also show failure to resist an impulse or temptation to perform the addicted behaviours. However, both addictions are also different in other aspects, which should be considered during assessment, prevention and treatment phases. For instance, the Internet is highly accessible with low costs as compared to drugs. The Internet is also often viewed more positively because of its wide acceptability in society. Thus, abstinence is possible either only temporarily or not effective at all.

Whether Internet addiction should be included in the *Diagnostic and Statistical Manual of Mental Disorders* (DSM-5) is yet to be confirmed. Many researchers and clinicians are still discussing whether Internet addiction can be classified as one of the impulse control disorders or whether it is merely a behavioural observation of many other types of mental disorders (e.g., depression and anxiety). Despite the ongoing debates, the prevalence of Internet addiction has caught the attention of many practitioners worldwide. Thus, it is important for us to look into prevention and intervention strategies before the phenomenon grows.

INTERNET ADDICTION AMONG CHILDREN AND YOUNG PERSONS

The prevalence of Internet addiction varies across countries and samples (Ko et al., 2012; Kuss, Griffiths, Karila & Billieux, 2014). For instance, 0.8% of adolescents in Italy and 26.4% of adolescent students in Hong Kong were considered to be addicted to the Internet. Studies conducted in China, Taiwan and South Korea also reported different prevalence estimates between 1.6% and 21%. In Singapore, 17.1% of adolescents were reported to use the Internet more than five hours daily (Mythily, Qiu & Winslow, 2008).

One possible reason for such vast differences in prevalence rates is the usage of different classification criteria. Various instruments, assessment tools and cut-off criteria are utilised in different research studies, making it challenging to compare the prevalence statistics across studies. For the purpose of illustration, this chapter will only focus on Young's Internet Addiction Test (IAT). Notwithstanding, this is not the best tool for Internet addiction assessment. More research studies are required to further conceptualise and assess the construct of Internet addiction.

In 2014, we conducted a research study comprising 3,319 students in secondary schools, junior colleges and polytechnics (Tan et al., 2015). The IAT was utilised to assess the extent of Internet addiction among adolescents in Singapore. Based on the classification method, 1.9% of adolescents reported having significant problems with Internet use. On the other hand, a relatively higher proportion of adolescents (34.4%) reported having occasional problems with Internet use. This suggests that Internet addiction might be an emerging phenomenon among adolescents in Singapore.

WARNING SIGNS OF INTERNET ADDICTION

So, how do we know if a person is developing Internet addiction, or at risk of it? Internet addiction is often not developed overnight. Various warning signs may be noticed by their immediate family members and friends. These include, but are not limited to:

- Excessive use of the Internet – People at risk use the Internet for many hours every day, which significantly affects their daily functioning. They are on their Internet-enabled devices almost all the time and often describe themselves as having lost their sense of time.

- Preoccupation with the Internet – The Internet is viewed as a very important aspect in their lives. Their minds are always occupied with the idea of being connected to the Internet, even when they are offline. They will always make attempts to check on things happening online.

- Withdrawal symptoms – When they are not connected to the Internet, they will show signs of anger, tension and/or depression. For instance, they may kick up a fuss because the Internet connection is too slow, hindering their connection to the virtual world. Some may also verbally protest at the removal of the computer or Internet-related devices.

- They are usually unable to control the amount of time spent on the Internet. When people ask about their online use, they can get overly sensitive and act out upon the questioning.

- Upon resuming their Internet use, they quickly experience a change of mood, typically a sense of calm and cheerfulness. This can be drastically different from how they behave offline.

- Tolerance symptoms – They have the urge to use better computer equipment or devices. They may complain about their current Internet connection speed and demand for a faster one. They also need more Internet time to achieve their desired mood, resulting in them staying online longer than intended.

- Because of excessive use, they may lack adequate rest. Many may have sleep issues as they often go to bed only at late hours. Such unhealthy sleep patterns can also be linked to poor self-care and weight loss/gain. Physical health problems, such as eye strain and back and wrist pains, can arise due to long hours of maintaining the same body posture while engaged on the devices.
- Long hours of Internet use can significantly affect social connections with others. They spend less time with family and friends just to continue staying on the Internet. School and work quality will also start to deteriorate. They may be insistent on using the Internet despite family conflicts or academic failures.

REASONS ADOLESCENTS ARE MORE AT RISK

Many research findings have shown that adolescents have a higher risk of developing Internet addiction. Various possible reasons have been offered to explain why adolescents are more at risk of Internet addiction (Beard, 2011; Greenfield, 2011).

First of all, adolescence is a period in which individuals have to deal with a lot of new challenges and difficulties. One of the most important psychosocial developments in adolescents is the search and formation of an identity. While it could be carried out through social interactions in the real world, many teenagers find it attractive to explore their identities in the virtual world. For instance, they are able to try different personas or characters in online games, which will in turn help to develop their own identities. In addition, the freedom of expressing their own identities in their social profiles can be another contributing factor. They can selectively choose to present their more favourable characteristics to others online.

As part of identity formation, adolescents also like to experience new things in life. Given that the content on the Internet is constantly updated and extremely interesting, the medium itself is already attractive to young people. Therefore, it is not uncommon to hear them describing certain online activities as "fun" and "cool" just because it is something new. The Internet can also be seen as a more convenient medium to try out things that are not legal in the real world. Being able to access pornography online or visit virtual casinos to gamble are two avenues that some adolescents may explore.

Moreover, the interactions online are usually accompanied by rapid responses and instant rewards. With a simple scroll and click, individuals can immediately receive tons of desired content from the Internet. One post on their Facebook or Instagram account can easily attract numerous "likes" and comments from their social circles. This immediate reward system directly reinforces the action of staying online.

The Internet can serve as an interactive platform for adolescents to communicate and form meaningful relationships with others. It is less anxiety-provoking and easier to communicate in this well-controlled environment. They may also experience peer modelling and pressure to engage in various online activities. For instance, if their friends are playing a certain online game, they are expected to play it together in order to stay connected with them. Likewise, by browsing the social networking sites, they can keep themselves updated about their friends' status at their convenience. This can prevent them from being isolated from their social circles.

The Internet is also addictive because of the secondary benefits that young people can gain. When adolescents face life challenges or interpersonal difficulties with others, the Internet can become a psychological escape that distracts them from such situations. They can experience pleasure and relief by avoiding the anxiety-provoking situation or life difficulty. However, as they do not have a chance to learn a better way of coping with such situations, it is very likely that they will face a similar problem in the future. This will in turn form a vicious circle, which will increase their use of the Internet and they become even more isolated from the real world.

Lastly, the wide level of acceptability and availability of Internet technologies in our culture can be another reason why adolescents are attracted to the Internet. Personal computers and Internet-enabled mobile phones are so prevalent and affordable that most people can easily own one nowadays. There are new Internet-enabled devices introduced in the market every year. In order to be part of the mainstream, one needs to be connected to the Internet.

OTHER MENTAL HEALTH ISSUES ASSOCIATED WITH INTERNET ADDICTION

Internet addiction often does not happen by itself. Many researchers and clinicians have repeatedly observed the co-occurrence of various mental disorders and issues with Internet addiction. Ko and colleagues (2012) have conducted a literature review to illustrate various coexisting psychiatric disorders, which include attention-deficit hyperactivity disorder, depression, hostility and social anxiety disorder.

In addition, our local study also supported the correlation between Internet addiction and adolescents' psychosocial wellbeing (Tan et al., 2015). By administering the Strengths and Difficulties Questionnaire, we found that adolescents who reported having more problems with Internet use (i.e., occasional and significant problems) are more likely to also have issues with their psychosocial wellbeing. Specifically, they scored higher on the hyperactive-inattention, emotional, conduct and peer problems subscales as compared to the average Internet users.

ATTENTION DEFICIT HYPERACTIVITY DISORDER (ADHD)

ADHD symptoms have been frequently found to be associated with Internet addiction. Young people with ADHD always report being easily bored. When they are engaged on the Internet, they are usually provided with rapid responses and immediate rewards. They are also able to multitask by opening multiple windows and be engaged on all of them at the same time. These Internet features can help to provide heightened stimulation, which in turn reduce their sense of boredom.

Moreover, another core symptom reported in ADHD is being impulsive. Individuals with ADHD have deficits in self-control, which may result in difficulties controlling Internet use.

DEPRESSION

Often, the Internet provides a safe and less threatening environment for individuals to escape from difficulties in the real world. If adolescents experience depressive symptoms, they may engage in the virtual world which is more controllable and pleasurable. They can decide which Internet applications they want to go to. Online entertainment and games can also provide temporary relief from their difficult situations.

HOSTILITY AND AGGRESSION

Adolescents with Internet addiction are more likely to display aggressive behaviours and vice versa. This could be because individuals who display aggressive acts might experience interpersonal conflicts, quarrels, rejection or isolation from others. Therefore, they choose to engage in the virtual world as a form of escape and way of coping. In addition, the perceived anonymity of the Internet could "encourage" them to express hostility and violence without restriction. Such behaviours are often observed on various social networking sites and in online gaming.

SOCIAL ANXIETY AND LACK OF INTERPERSONAL SKILLS

Individuals with a lack of interpersonal skills often face challenges in initiating and maintaining face-to-face relationships. Thus, the virtual world could be one possible outlet they can go to in order to prevent being isolated and lonely. Online social interactions are often described as easier and less threatening because of the lack of nonverbal cues. By communicating and interacting online, they can choose to present only certain aspects of their personalities and mask undesirable ones. Such engagement can reduce the possibility of being judged, in turn positively reinforcing Internet use and eventually substituting for face-to-face relationships.

Notwithstanding, studies conducted to examine these associations are usually cross-sectional studies. Therefore, causality relationships are difficult to establish. We are not sure whether the psychological issues are the cause or effect of Internet addiction, or whether they are mutually reinforcing. Nevertheless, the awareness of such co-occurrences can be helpful in various prevention and intervention strategies.

PREVENTION AND MANAGEMENT

CASE STUDY

After returning from work, Mrs Lee saw her son, Kelvin, playing computer games in his room. He was still in his school uniform and had been playing since he came back from school. He was always on his computer – playing games, surfing the net and chatting with his friends throughout the day and night. She warned him to stop playing while she was preparing dinner. "Just a while more," Kelvin replied.

After she had finished dinner preparation, Mrs Lee was furious because Kelvin was still on his computer. She stomped into his room and switched off the electrical supply. "Can you just stop playing and go for a bath? The only thing you know is to play computer games and talk to your so-called friends online!" she shouted. Kelvin was upset because he was about to finish his game. "You don't understand! What else can I do since I am alone at home all the time!" he yelled. At the same time, he shoved his mother out of the room and slammed the door. Mrs Lee was heartbroken and felt lost.

The case study above illustrates one typical example of how parent-child relationships can be affected because of Internet use. Various prevention strategies can be implemented to better manage behaviour and improve quality of life in the family.

- Establish house rules on the pattern and frequency of Internet use at a young age. It is important for children to understand structures, routines and limits. For instance, parents can set aside certain amounts of time that children can use the computers/devices, or disallow them to be used during dinner.

- Be firm and consistent on the rules and boundaries. Parents can discuss with their children to decide together on the reward and punishment system for following such rules.

- Be a role model. Imagine a situation where parents ask their children to stop playing computer games while they are still engaged on their iPads. Be serious about the rules and remember to apply them to everyone in the family.
- Provide understanding and empathy towards children. Whenever there is conflict at home regarding Internet use, remember to stay calm and be constructive. Scolding and hitting is the last thing that you would want to do. Be a good listener to understand what they are going through. Keep a protected time daily if you can, to communicate and ensure basic needs for love and companionship are met.
- Cultivate interest in recreational activities and sports. Instead of being engaged on the computer and the Internet, parents can offer substitutes to encourage them to take part in other activities. These can promote a healthier and more balanced lifestyle, and at the same time instil a sense of pride if they achieve something in the activities. It will be even better if the family is engaged in a similar activity together.
- Try to understand what technologies young people are interested in. It can be in the form of social networking sites or online games. While it will be challenging because technologies advance rapidly, it is helpful to have some common topics with the child. This can help in the parent-child bond and show them that you care and understand them.

CONCLUSION

Internet technology was developed to aid human life. The ability to stay connected and interact with others significantly improves our social interactions and provides emotional support for many individuals. The Internet is also a source of knowledge, helping us discover new ideas and be exposed to diverse cultures in the world. Its entertainment features (e.g., online games and movies) are often beneficial as an activity to de-stress. Online gaming, in particular, may also help to develop certain skills, such as hand-eye coordination and integration of perceptual information. However, newer studies have suggested it can also impact negatively on specific aspects of learning. Therefore, the Internet should be used wisely and with caution in order for us to enjoy its true benefits while protecting ourselves from its negative consequences.

ONLINE GAMING ADDICTION

Jayanthi d/o Manohar
Ray Chua Swee Boon
Dr Huu Kim Le

CASE STUDY

Bryan grew up as an only child with his father, a very successful career man and his mother, a housewife who spent most of her time with Bryan. He grew up feeling very satisfied with the amount of care and attention that he received from his parents, and was very attached to them, especially his mother.

When he started schooling, Bryan had a lot of difficulty adjusting, crying and isolating himself from his teachers and peers. This continued throughout his primary school years. Always keeping to himself, he did not make any friends and his social skills were very poor. His problems further worsened when his parents divorced when he was nine. His father left the household and his mother had to start working. Depending on his parents for most of his life, their separation came down hard on him and he found himself feeling even lonelier.

At the age of 12, his cousins introduced him to online games. His previous experience of games was limited to educational games which he would play occasionally with his mother. However, online games were a game changer for him, with its multiple features and realistic experiences. He quickly found his favorites, *Counter-Strike*, a first-person shooter game and *World of Warcraft*, an online role playing game. His frequency of gaming started increasing and he ended up playing games daily. His social circle also found a new breath of life as he increasingly communicated with fellow gamers online. Slowly, he grew more attracted to the virtual world, where he could find fun and enjoyment, where he could feel happy and excited and where he had people he could talk to.

Now at 15, his mother has brought him to the Institute of Mental Health's National Addictions Management Service (NAMS) due to concerns that Bryan may be suffering from online gaming addiction. Bryan's relationship with online games had grown over the years. His need for gaming time had increased, sometimes even skipping school and CCA to get his dose of online games. His performance and results in school were worsening as he did not have much time to study or do his homework with his gaming schedule. His late night play also resulted in him falling asleep in class and teachers raising complaints to his mother. His relationship with his mother was getting strained with his frequent lies on his activities and whereabouts and he rarely took his eyes off the screen to communicate and spend time with his mother. Their relationship was reduced to her constant nagging at him to stop gaming and his expressions of frustration at her when she attempts to remove the computer away from him. His mother who had once been the apple of his eye was now an impediment to his gaming, which had gradually taken centre stage in his life.

UNDERSTANDING ONLINE GAMES

Online games are electronic games that are played over the Internet. They allow gamers to play either competitively against other gamers or cooperatively with others to achieve game objectives. With the increasing availability of fast home Internet access, online games have seen a sharp increase in popularity.

There are many features of online games that make these games attractive and addictive to gamers. Regular game events are held to entice gamers to play for greater rewards. These events are often held at times where gamers are likely to have free time to play, such as during public holidays or school holidays. Once gamers miss these game events, they might not have a second opportunity to obtain these desired game rewards. Online games often provide immediate reinforcement while the gamer goes about achieving game objectives. Gamers who play online shooters (action games) receive "praise" from the game whenever they are able to execute skillful moves. They also receive social reinforcement when the game broadcasts the gamer's achievements to other players.

Online games are also designed to be social activities. Gamers often group together into "guilds" or "clans" in order to pool their efforts to achieve common game objectives. Common social motivations include involving oneself in the game because a friend asks for help to obtain a certain game reward or because friends need more players to help fill a team. Finally, gamers are motivated to play in order to obtain a high rank in "game ladders". Game ladders are listings of top players in the game and players are ranked typically by their skill or their in-game achievements. Gamers who are high ranked typically feel a sense of great achievement and also social recognition from other players. Players can also take part in gaming competitions organised by gaming companies and win prize money ranging from thousands of dollars for local competitions to millions of dollars in top international competitions.

ONLINE GAMING ADDICTION

CASE STUDY

Kevin: Dad, you have to be kidding me!

Dad: (keeps silent, reading newspaper)

Kevin: Dad!!! Where is it?

Dad: I already told you.

Kevin: Told me what!

Dad: (after a long pause, speaking in a calm, stern tone)
        I told you that if you didn't keep to our agreement
        one more time, I will have to confiscate it.

Kevin: Yeah but...

Dad: No more buts Kevin. I've had enough of your excuses. This time I'm not giving in.

Kevin: Dad!! You can't do this to me now. They will be waiting for me.

Dad: I don't care. This conversation is over.

Kevin: Nooooo. Don't do this to me, Dad. Pleaseeee. Just one last chance. I promise I will keep to our agreement. Just one last time.

Dad: No Kevin. You've had too many chances.

Kevin: Dad! Pleaseeee! I'm already late. Just give it to me for a while.

Dad: (keeps silent)

Realising that his dad was not going to give in, Kevin lets out a grunt, kicks the sofa and stomps into his room, banging the door behind him. A while later,

Kevin: Dad. (holding onto a knife)

Dad: Kevin. What do you think you are doing? Put that down.

Kevin: Give it back to me.

Dad: Kevin. I'm asking you to put that down.

Kevin: NO! If you don't give it back, I swear I'm going to kill you. GIVE IT BACK TO ME!

Dad: Ok Kevin. You put the knife down first and I will give it back to you.

Kevin: NO! You give it back to me first! (gripping onto the knife tightly)

Dad: Ok, ok relax! (hurries into his room and takes the keyboard out of the cupboard)

Still holding on to the knife, Kevin snatches the keyboard while staring at his father. He then heads to his room with the knife in his hand and his face lights up as the gaming screen turns on.

....

In the most recent edition of the *Diagnostic Statistical Manual of Mental Health* (DSM-5) used by mental health professionals to diagnose mental health disorders, there is an online gaming disorder that has been proposed for further study by mental health researchers. This condition is known as Internet Gaming Disorder (IGD; American Psychiatric Association, 2013). IGD is defined as the persistent and recurrent use of the Internet to engage in games, often with other players, leading to distress or impairment in their everyday functioning. Characteristics of this disorder include preoccupation with gaming, withdrawal symptoms, need for increasing amounts of gaming in order to be fulfilled, conflict with others and deception over gaming, inability to control the behaviour despite problems, loss of interest in non-gaming activities and using gaming to relieve a negative mood.

Based on the measurement items similar to the diagnostic criteria for IGD, studies conducted around the globe present that 8-12% of adolescents who participated in research can be considered being addicted to games (Choo et al., 2015). According to one study carried out with 2,998 primary and secondary students in Singapore (Choo et al., 2010), about one in eleven (8.7%) youth surveyed were found to be pathological gamers who endorsed five or more pathological symptoms of video gaming.

Current research also suggests that there are various risk factors for online gaming addiction. DSM-5 identifies two types of risk factors: environmental and physiological. For environmental factors, a Singaporean study (Choo et al., 2010) found that having a video game system in the bedroom increases the risk of gaming addiction. For physiological factors, both DSM-5 and Khoo's study note that males are at higher risk. In addition to gender, the following were also found in the study to be risk factors for developing gaming addiction:

- Gamers who spend more time on online games and visit LAN centres frequently are at higher risk. Addicted gamers spend an average of 37 hours on gaming per week whilst non-addicted gamers spend an average of 18 hours per week. Gamers often visit LAN centres as a group and they could be encouraged by their friends to continue even if they wish to stop. In addition, gamers could also extend gaming time when enticed by attractive LAN centre promotions and package deals.

- Gamers who are underachieving academically are also at higher risk. Gamers who are unable to obtain a sense of achievement and significance in real world arenas such as the classroom or the sports field look towards gaming achievements to meet this need.

- Gamers who are impulsive and lack social skills are also at higher risk. Gamers who are impulsive would have greater challenges in controlling their urges to game. Such gamers are also likely to find real world commitments such as work or studies to be much less stimulating as compared to the exciting world of online gaming. Gamers with poor social skills and awareness often find that life is much easier without having to communicate face-to-face with others. Online communication is less demanding on a person's social abilities and these gamers could be using online applications such as games as an alternative medium to meet their social needs.

- Gamers with poor parent-child relationships are at higher risk of online gaming addiction. Strong family relationships act as a protective factor for many mental health challenges, including online gaming addiction. When the parent-child relationship breaks down, parents lose the ability to positively influence their children towards a balanced use of online gaming.

According to the DSM-5, IGD has the same clinical features as substance addictions (American Psychiatric Association, 2013). Studies have shown that a gaming addict's brain can be triggered in the same way as in drug addiction.

When dealing with a child suffering from IGD, the greatest struggle a parent may face is when they have to restrict the child's access to the technological device. This may set the child into withdrawal symptoms ranging from irritability, low mood, aggression and even acts of self-harm. Behaviours may even stretch to posing threats or stealing, just to get their fix.

Online games can meet needs on such a fundamental level that the difference between reality and the virtual world can be blurred. In fact, a person who has difficulties in real life, such as failures in achievement, social status, competition and relating to others, may find that these needs can be more easily met in the virtual world. Many who have found solace in online gaming have a reduced desire and capability to function in real life. Studies have shown that online gaming addiction can lead to poor performance in school, the person becoming more withdrawn, in turn leading to neglect of family and friends. However, in these gamers' online worlds, they inhabit characters that are powerful, boast belts of achievements and have very active social lives.

This blurring of the virtual and real world often leads to disagreements between the gamer and his family. Families might find themselves set against their child's arguments of their potential and success in the virtual world. The increasing realism of games makes one perceive that they are able to get the full experience of living from the comfort of their armchair. Parents may resort to measures like drastically reducing their computer access or removing it as a whole, which would further strengthen the child's belief that the virtual world is a better world to live in.

The importance of the online gaming world increases as their relationships in the real world become more conflictual. The child gets increasingly dependent on the gaming world and may even feel pressured to maintain and stay on top in this world. The persistence of the online gaming world (game continues even in the absence of the gamer) creates a feeling of anxiousness when the gamer is not online. Gamers would frequently neglect their sleep, meal times and even hygiene to ensure that they are able to succeed in their gaming world.

This dedication to online games can extend beyond their gaming time when they constantly think or fantasise about the games. Online games require lots of planning and strategy and hence a gamer may spend his offline time strategising his next gaming venture or thinking about ways to sharpen his skills. Interest, concentration and attention span on any other activity such as hobbies or studies greatly diminished as the gamer gets his dopamine fix from the games.

Subjecting your body to long hours on a computer chair with your eyes glued to the screen with hands and fingers in continuous rapid, repetitive movements can also take a toll on your body. Symptoms can range from body aches to more serious conditions such as carpal tunnel syndrome and deep vein thrombosis. Death from online games have also been making the news with the recent story of a man found dead in a Taiwanese cafe after a three-day gaming binge.

SMARTPHONE GAMING ADDICTION

Another trend that has been of growing interest is smartphone gaming addiction. Smartphone technology is one that is rapidly growing with an increasing base of customers who are intent on getting their hands on the latest smartphone models. In comparison with other technological devices, it has the most usage given its ease of portability and multiple functions. Game developers have harnessed this trend by developing games that are compatible with the smartphone. Games like *Clash of Clans*, *Candy Crush* and *Hearthstone* are some of the games that are popular with smartphone users.

While it is common to think that all games operate on the same mechanism, these smartphone games come with very distinctive features that set it apart from massively multiplayer online role playing games (MMORPGs) which are well known for their role playing functions, fantasy themes and multiplayer facilities.

The addiction to smartphone games can be explained with:

- The simplicity of the game utilises very little cognitive resource thus appealing to different ages and educational groups.
- The games create an illusion of control by tapping on your urge to find patterns (e.g., candies in varied shapes and colours in *Candy Crush*) in the game. While finding patterns can be gratifying, the user receives reinforcements on a variable reinforcement schedule thus increasing the addictive property of the game.
- In comparison to MMORPGs, less time is required to play at each level of smartphone games, thus allowing the user to start on the game in small gaps of times (e.g., in between breaks, while waiting for the bus, etc.) that he has without having to set aside a specific amount of time for it.
- The games are built to improve your chances of winning with each failed turn, keeping the user engaged with "near-

win" moments. This feature keeps the user motivated to keep trying.

- Many apps and games are free to start off with, but game developers have ways to monetise these games by allowing users to buy extra "lives" or special features. For some people who have difficulty controlling their smartphone gameplay they may find themselves spending a lot more money than they had intended and in some cases end up in financial debt.

Another potential problem with smartphone users are physical complaints. Repetitive strain injuries may develop from frequent use of the thumb or fingers due to the relatively small size of the screen, which places joints of the hand at unnatural positions. Also, people may develop poor posture of the neck and spine due to looking down at their screen too much. In some cases, people may suffer accidents from not looking where they are walking or driving because they were not paying enough attention to their surroundings.

PREVENTION

Singapore has one of the highest Internet penetration rates in the world. Together with the increasing advancement of technology and ease of access to it, online gaming has gained increasing popularity over the years, especially amongst adolescents. While gaming does have its benefits, it can quickly reveal its harm if it is not used in moderation.

In 2011, South Korea passed the Shutdown law, which

forbids children under the age of 16 from playing online video games from 12.00 am to 6.00 am. This was a government attempt to address the increasing prevalence of online gaming addiction amongst the young as parental attempts to control their children's use of online games turn futile.

When a child crosses the line to online gaming addiction, professional help should be sought to undergo treatment for Internet gaming disorder. However, plenty of preventive measures can be taken to ensure that the child does not cross this line.

- Monitor the amount of time spent on online games – The extent of online gaming can be masked by the child's practical use of the technological device. As schools increasingly weave in e-learning into their curriculum, the computer becomes an integral part of their learning process. Hence, it is important to understand the child's usage of the computer and the actual amount of time spent on online games. Monitoring software has made this possible especially in households where both parents are working. Having an accurate measure of the amount of time spent on online games prevents unnecessary arguments on the topic.

- Set a limit – The American Academy of Paediatrics recommends a screen time guideline of no more than two hours a day for school-aged children and teenagers. It is important that every child's need for computer usage is individually understood, taking into consideration their schoolwork or any other activities. The type of game played would also be a guide in understanding the amount of time the child may require in a single seating. With this understanding, the parents can then set a realistic time limit that will be well suited for the child. What is more important would be for the parents to reinforce this limit and help the child to stay within the time limit set.

- Encourage a healthy relationship with the computer – The computer's location and the rules for computer usage have an impact on the child's long term relationship with the computer. Placing the computer in the hall, in a well-lit place allows the child to understand that there can be no secrecy in the usage of the computer. It also allows the child to stay connected with family members and their activities. Further, a consistent practice of taking breaks while using the computer reduces the risk of physical ailments such as eye strain and body aches. Parents can best inculcate these values in the child by being a good role model and following the rules set for computer usage.

- Build strong familial relationships – Studies have shown that having strong familial relationships is a protective factor against online gaming addiction. Fostering a bond through common activities such as meal times and board games enhances the quality of relationships. Adopting an open and understanding approach in communication would also help to develop trust and strengthen the relationship.

- Understand the child's needs – Adolescence can be quite tumultuous as a young person struggles to find his own identity amidst pressure from school, peers and family. Adjusting to peer culture while trying to achieve academic excellence can leave many feeling stressed or even suffer from low self-esteem. Having someone who can lend them a listening ear without being judgmental allows the child to feel understood and comforted. Parents can connect with their friends and school to get an understanding of any difficulties their child may be facing. Appropriate help should be sought should the child be suffering from any underlying problems.

- Explore the child's strengths and interests – While your child struggles to find his identity through adolescence, focusing on his strengths and interests would give him a sense of direction and grounding. A child may not understand where his strengths lie and it would help if they were highlighted to him. Providing him with the opportunities to pursue his interests would give him more purpose and meaning in life.

SOCIAL MEDIA USAGE AND TEXTING

Dr Melvyn Zhang Weibin

....

CASE STUDY

Sarah is 16 and has not been attending school for four months. She is in her last year of secondary school and is expected to take her GCE 'O' Level examinations in a few months. She spends much of her time at home using her computer and her smartphone. Her parents are very concerned about her studies and have decided to call the Institute of Mental Health's National Addiction Management Service (NAMS) helpline. She has been referred to see an adolescent addiction specialist at the clinic.

During the consultation with the specialist, Sarah reveals that her mood has been low since the start of the school year. She finds herself having no interest in her studies. She says that her parents do not understand her difficulties and they wrongfully accuse her of having an addiction to the computer and smartphone. She admits that she spends relatively large amounts of time online, averaging from eight to ten hours per day. She shares that she has several social media accounts, ranging from Facebook to Twitter, and she has been using these social media accounts to communicate with her friends, given that she is now not at school. Apart from using social media to communicate with her peers, she has also been actively using social media to learn more about what her friends are doing. She attests to spending a large proportion of her time on Instagram, looking at the photos that her friends have posted.

She acknowledges that she also spends a large quantity of her time using her smartphone. She claims that using a smartphone device is much more enjoyable than interacting with her family and friends in a real life environment. When her smartphone was broken, she experienced significant restlessness and felt that she had lost "the entire world". She realises that her usage of social media and the smartphone has affected her ability to concentrate on academic work, and shares that she had previously attempted to cut down, but failed.

Given the history shared by Sarah, she was referred for counselling by the addiction counsellor. The adolescent specialist also made a follow-up appointment with her to review her mood symptoms, to determine if she might benefit from a course of low dose antidepressant for her low mood and reduction in interest.

SOCIAL MEDIA ADDICTION

The case example clearly illustrates an adolescent who is addicted to social media usage and has associated smartphone addiction as well. Her addiction with social media has led to a corresponding psychiatric issue, which might be that of a depressive disorder.

Social media refers to social networking as well as blogging sites. Examples include Facebook, Instagram, Twitter and Tumblr. More recently, social media sites such as Ask.Fm and Snapchat have been increasingly popular. Social media sites appeal to adolescents as it helps them get connected to their friends. Social media sites provide youths with instant feedback from friends and help them to keep themselves updated with the latest trends worldwide. In addition, for some adolescents, it helps provide them with validation and gives them a sense of value, based on the number of "likes" they gain from their posts online. For some, it provides them with a safe haven to ask questions, without being identified by their peers. As keeping in touch in real time and on-the-go is very important to adolescents, most young people find it easier to use their smartphones rather than computers to connect socially with their friends. Thus this chapter refers to how young people are hooked on social media platforms via the Internet or smartphone.

Recent studies done in Singapore highlighted that a relatively large proportion of Singaporean youths are addicted to the Internet, as well as to social media. A study done by a group of researchers at Singapore Polytechnic has highlighted that the average number of hours Singaporean youths spend online daily has increased from 4.8 hours to 5.5 hours (Sim, 2013). Most of the youths spend their time online on the following activities, with the most common usage ranked right on top:

- Browsing through web-based contents
- Viewing photos and videos shared by others
- Replying to others and commenting on social media posts made by others
- Chatting online
- Posting new content

A further study done more recently by a team at Singapore Polytechnic (Hio, 2015) also showed how usage of the Internet and social media has changed over the years. Previously, in 2012, the usage of the social media website, Instagram, ranked low amongst the youth. However, as much as 50% of youths are currently using this social media website when re-surveyed in 2014. It is essential to determine trends associated with usage of social media, as it will have a corresponding impact on intervention strategies. Prior research has also shown that youths with higher levels of wellbeing tend to spend less time online, as compared to those with lower levels of wellbeing (Sim, 2013). Apart from the association between wellbeing and the number of hours spent online, it has also been demonstrated that levels of happiness have a correlation and association with the number of hours spent online. Those who spend fewer hours online tend to score higher on the happiness index.

With the existing pervasiveness of the Internet and smartphones amongst youths, it is not hard to recognise the fact that younger youths tend to prefer to communicate with their friends and even their family members using social media.

CHARACTERISTICS OF SOCIAL MEDIA ADDICTION AND DIAGNOSIS

Internet addiction and smartphone addiction fall under the category of behavioural addiction. In general, these disorders have the following features in common:

- Preoccupation with the particular behaviour
- Occurrence of withdrawal symptoms when the behaviour is hindered
- The need to spend increasing amounts of time indulging in the particular behaviour
- Previous unsuccessful efforts at reducing the undesired behaviour
- Continuation of the behaviour despite its negative consequences
- Psychosocial impairments arising from the behaviour itself

It should be noted that even though Internet addiction and smartphone addiction are behavioural addictions well researched into, the current diagnostic system (DSM-5) has included only a proposed diagnostic classification that is not part of the formal diagnosable disorders. Social media, in itself, is a subset of Internet and smartphone addiction, and would share the above-mentioned characteristics. There are no available guidelines currently to diagnose an individual with social media addiction. We could assume the commonalities between Internet and smartphone addiction and social media addiction. The above criteria should alert clinicians to a high possibility of an underlying social media addictive behaviour.

Very often, clinicians and researchers rely on a standardised questionnaire to help them in the diagnosis of these forms of addiction. For diagnosis of Internet addiction, much of the current evidence points towards the usage of Young's Internet Addiction Test. The Internet Addiction Test proposed and validated by Young has 20 items on the scale, and a score of 80-100 points on the score would diagnose a person with Internet addiction. With regard to smartphone addiction, researchers in Korea have proposed the smartphone addiction scale and they have just validated the scale amongst a total of 540 participants. The 10-item scale could help in the diagnosis of smartphone addiction. Some of the items on the scale include questions assessing disturbance of adaptive functioning, as well as characteristic tolerance and withdrawal symptoms. In addition, the scale also looks into virtual life orientation, which is how the individual perceives the impact of the smartphone on his or her life.

With regard to social media addiction, research into validated questionnaires is much in its infancy. Recent research has only looked into the validation of a Facebook addiction scale, known as the Bergen Facebook addiction scale. This scale consists of 18 items, with at least three items looking into different aspects of the addictive behaviour. These areas include that of salience, mood modification, tolerance, withdrawal, conflict and relapse. Importantly, this particular scale has been validated in some countries, such as Thailand. Even though the scale is specific to Facebook, the items could easily be generalised to other social media platforms and hence, such a scale would be of use for clinicians who have been asked to determine whether a person has an addiction to social media.

Below is an overview of the Bergen Facebook addiction scale and the significant items within each of the subsections:

Salience	Spend a lot of time thinking about Facebook or planned use of Facebook
Tolerance	Feel an urge to use Facebook more and more
Mood modification	Use Facebook in order to forget about personal problems
Relapse	Tried to cut down on the use of Facebook without success
Withdrawal	Become restless or troubled if prohibited from using Facebook
Conflict	Use Facebook so much that it has had a negative impact on a job or studies

COMORBIDITIES ASSOCIATED WITH EXCESSIVE SOCIAL MEDIA USAGE

Previous research has looked in depth into the association between Internet addiction and psychiatric comorbidity (Ho, 2014). The authors searched previous published literature and included eight studies with a cumulative total of 1,641 patients diagnosed with Internet addiction for analysis. That research highlighted an association between Internet addiction and several other psychiatric comorbidities, including alcohol abuse, Attention Deficit Hyperactivity Disorder (ADHD) as well as anxiety disorders. This means that people with Internet addiction are predisposed to the other disorders as mentioned above. There is an approximately two to three times increased incidence of acquiring the aforementioned psychiatric disorders.

Whilst there has been much work looking into the associated psychiatric comorbidity between Internet addiction and psychiatric disorder, there is a relative paucity of existing studies looking into the association between social media usage and comorbid psychiatric disorders. The existing studies have largely looked into the association between Facebook addiction and psychiatric disorders.

Some of the previously published studies have highlighted an association between Facebook addiction and the following:

- Development of poor emotion regulation skills
- Higher incidence of acquiring substance and non-substance addiction
- Lower scores on subjective happiness
- Neuroticism and extraversion personality traits
- Higher emotional exhaustion
- Higher incidence of depressive disorder

Apart from the above associated psychiatric disorders, it should be noted that youths usually have no issue with accepting strangers as their friends on social media. This might be an issue, as youths tend to be more vulnerable to potential exploitation. Hence, there is a need to educate youths on how to use and navigate social media usage safely in today's world.

Also, in view of the fact that youths are able to share their personal information on social media websites, it is pertinent to educate youths about the vulnerabilities involved. There is a chance that their privacy might be violated. Youths do need to demonstrate an understanding of this. In addition, social media usage also opens up the dangers of cyberbullying. This will be addressed in another chapter in this guidebook, but it is another area where youths might be vulnerable. Youths who are exposed to cyberbullying and threats tend to develop psychiatric disorders.

SOCIAL MEDIA USAGE AND ITS POTENTIAL BENEFITS

Much of what has been shared about social media has shown that it has potentially more negative implications than positive advantages for users. However, recent research has shown that social media could also be an invaluable tool in certain situations.

Whilst the excessive usage of social media has been linked to various psychiatric comorbidities, the appropriate use of social media could help to engage youths and provide intervention and education about health-related behaviours. Other researchers have also managed to tap into social media and understand more about adolescents' perceptions and misconceptions towards substances. Through the use of social media, such understanding would help in the formulation of appropriate interventions for youths.

PREVENTION STRATEGIES

To date, there has yet to be much research evidence and literature purporting the ideal strategies for social media addiction intervention. Whilst help could be sought from national addiction management centers and cyber wellness centers, it would be ideal if parents could work together with their youths to engage them in activity scheduling and more meaningful activities. Parents could help restrict the amount of time that youths spend online via the usage of timers as well. There is currently a variety of smartphone applications that help parents monitor their children's usage of the devices on the android platform. Understanding which applications young people use most commonly could help in terms of intervention. In addition, youths should be helped to understand the severity of their addiction. Other strategies might include setting restrictions on data utilisation usage in order to better manage the problem.

OTHER PROBLEMATIC ONLINE BEHAVIOURS: SHOPPING, GAMBLING, PORNOGRAPHY

Lawrence Tan Kok Kah

PROBLEMATIC ONLINE BEHAVIOURS

There is a host of addictive online behaviours that may greatly compromise the quality of a person's life if engaged in a compulsive fashion. This chapter will focus on three common ones: online shopping, pornography and gambling. Before jumping straight into the exploration of these behaviours, it is helpful to first look at what constitutes a behavioural addiction and how the online dimension can be a game changer in several ways.

The stories of Jane and Jill may be a helpful starting point for establishing a basic understanding of behavioural addictions and compulsive behaviours.

CASE STUDY

Jane is a single, 40-year-old sales executive who visits the online casino on a monthly basis. Each time, she takes special care and makes efforts to adhere to strict limits she sets on her gambling. This includes a loss and time limit of

300 dollars and three hours respectively. In order to help her stick to these safety limits, she sets an alarm on her mobile phone when she is at the online casino. It should also be noted that Jane is gainfully employed and can well afford the 300 dollars she spends monthly at the online casino.

CASE STUDY

Jill is a 15-year-old student was given a brand new laptop by her parents as a birthday present. With this laptop, she was able to freely access the wireless network her parents have subscribed to and found it tremendously convenient to go online and seek information as and when she requires. Initially it was purely for the purpose of schoolwork or on topics she was personally interested in (e.g., her favourite boy bands, pets or movies). Her online activities were compartmentalised in such a way that it did not affect the other aspects of her life and her wellbeing. Over time, Jill found herself spending more time searching and collecting data online. She got easily distracted and ended up following one pop-up link after another because she simply could not contain herself. It not only affected her ability to get her school projects done but also her level of self-care. She found herself hooked on the Internet and unable to tear herself away from her laptop screen even when it was way past her bedtime. She would wake up in the morning exhausted and be reluctant to go to school. She got into trouble in classes because of her tendency to fall asleep or be inattentive. She either felt too exhausted to focus or became distracted by thoughts about wanting to get back to her laptop again. She would even skip school from time to time for her online activities. The end of the semester saw a drastic drop in Jill's grades and her concerned form teacher arranged to meet her parents.

Let us pause for a moment and think about the stories of Jane and Jill. Who do you think has a problem? Jill's situation is obviously problematic, because her behaviour has disrupted her life and brought some degree of harm to herself. This brings us to the definition of an online behavioural addiction, a form of addiction that involves a compulsion to repeatedly perform a rewarding non-drug-related behaviour online despite negative consequences to the person's physical, mental, social, and/or financial well-being.

Jane and Jill's stories clearly illustrate how an online behaviour that has been historically seen as a vice (gambling) can become a rather healthy pastime when done under strict and safe control measures whereas a behaviour that is traditionally considered as educational and wholesome (seeking information) can turn out so wrong when engaged in a compulsive way. Jill's behaviour clearly illustrates traits of preoccupation, a continual engagement in behaviour despite negative consequences, a decline in both occupational and social functioning, and signs of emotional distress when disengaged from behaviour. Although not as clearly established as substance use disorder, we can clearly see from this example that any online behaviour, when left unchecked and carried to its extreme, can bring about serious problems.

A PROPOSED FRAMEWORK FOR ADDICTIVE ONLINE BEHAVIOURS

Having had some basic ideas of what constitutes a behavioural addiction, let us now look at how having an added online dimension can dramatically change the playing field. An interesting framework to utilise when we are looking at addictive online behaviours (e.g., online gambling or shopping) would be Grohol's model of pathological Internet use (Grohol, 2003) as mentioned in Chapter Two.

In this model, it is hypothesised that when new or existing Internet users stumble upon a new online activity (e.g., online shopping or gambling) which interests them, they enter a phase of enchantment where they get so drawn into the online activity that it takes centre stage in their lives for brief periods.

They may have obsessive thoughts about the activity and often experience some difficulty tearing themselves away. They may, to some extent, find themselves disengaging from the activities and socialisation which they used to enjoy in order to spend more time with their newfound online interest. Some users then progress to the next stage of disillusionment where the novelty of this new activity simply wears off; they are likely to swing from very frequent use or overuse to perhaps a stage where they simply want to take a break from the "overexposure" and avoid it completely.

Many of these users then go on to the next phase of normalisation where they are able to moderate their use of an activity to a point where they are able to skilfully strike a balance between an online activity and other aspects of their lives such that these activities become minimally disruptive.

There was a time when consumers were first introduced to online shopping websites like Qoo10 and Groupon a number of years ago. It was common for people to spend hours of their free time browsing the numerous items on sale and the attractive price tags that came with them.

They spent huge amounts of time looking through reviews, deciding which retailer they wanted to purchase from. These websites quickly went to the top of their "hit list". After making the purchase online, they would eagerly anticipate the items to be delivered with an overwhelming gratification that they had made a good deal.

Interestingly, as mentioned in Grohol's model, this phase did not last a long time for many of these consumers. Many of them gradually grew tired of looking at the same websites over and over again for the fun of it and the desire to simply buy something "interesting" over these platforms abated. They also got less and less excited over the delivery of certain items they have ordered to a point that they would forget certain items were still in transit and waiting to be delivered until the items actually appeared on their doorsteps.

Some of them even got so sick and tired of searching for, comparing and eventually buying items online that they deleted the applications for these platforms just to make space for other applications on their smartphones. Not long after, many of them were drawn into other interests in life, "abstaining" from shopping websites naturally for days and weeks. They may still check on those websites from time to time whenever they feel too lazy to go down to the mall; but they do not spend inordinate amounts of time on them and have very much become "access when in need" kind of users.

It seems like most users, when engaging with online activities that intrigue them, cruise past the initial enchantment, go on to disillusionment and finally reach a balanced phase as suggested by Grohol's model of Internet use. This is somewhat similar to how many people may have experimented with addictive behaviours like gambling or alcohol use at some point in their lives but only a small percentage go on to become pathological users.

Problematic Internet users, on the other hand, seem stuck in the first phase (enchantment phase) of the model and often require some form of assistance or intervention for them to move to the second and third stages, finding balance and integrating the online activity without disrupting other important areas of their lives. Let us now look at common types of online behaviours that, when not kept in check, can bring about problems in various areas of one's life and result in a serious decline of functioning.

COMPULSIVE ONLINE SHOPPING

According to Kellett & Bolton (2009), compulsive buying is experienced as an irresistible and uncontrollable urge, resulting in excessive, expensive and time-consuming retail activity which is commonly triggered by negative affectivity and results in gross social, personal and/or financial difficulties.

CASE STUDY

Meili, a 26-year-old sales executive, gets home from work most nights around 7.00 p.m. Once she is back home, her routine consists of having dinner, turning on the TV and spending a minimum of three to four hours online shopping (part surfing from one site to another, part purchasing products online, and a lot of time spent on Groupon and Qoo10). While it can deceptively look like a harmless hobby on the surface, it has become such a severe problem for Meili that she admits she is struggling with unmanageable credit card debts, and has a private P.O. Box to hide her card bills and online purchases from her parents who live with her.

We know for a fact that before online shopping was popularised, there were already compulsive shoppers who experience various dysfunctions in many areas of their lives and were using shopping as coping behaviour (much like compulsive gamblers and video gamers). How are these shoppers different from someone like Meili?

There are some key differences, according to Bourne (2015) on what leads a person to be addicted to stores in a shopping mall as compared to the person addicted to online shopping. The run-of-the-mill compulsive shopper "tends to have a relationship with salespeople, likes the tactile nature of the experience, the feel and touch and smell of it". The compulsive online shopper on the other hand, "can be very detached, and is often intrigued and drawn to the experience of rapidly clicking through sites like Groupon, Qoo10 or eBay to find the best deals. That's the adrenaline rush for them." Besides the adrenaline rush and sense of satisfaction over the discovery and securing of a good online deal on the one hand, there is also the fear and anxiety of missing or losing out on a "good deal" out there on the other hand.

Where exactly does a temporary preoccupation end and full-blown compulsive behaviour start? Using the behavioural addiction framework to help put things in perspective, it seems that compulsive shoppers get a sense of euphoria (or what we sometimes call a "high") or perhaps elicit feelings of escapism (over painful emotions or realities) and they constantly want to replicate that feeling over and over again despite negative consequences.

It is important, however, to note that not everyone engaging in compulsive behaviours or online behaviours are the same. Some are addicted to the various rituals of the behaviour (e.g., turning on the computer, logging onto certain webpages and going into certain mobile applications). The others are drawn into engaging in the behaviour over and over again because of the outcomes, such as a numbing effect on painful emotions and being able to create a parallel universe that is seemingly more desirable to be in than the real world.

When we look deeper into the issue, we may realise that online shoppers are not necessarily preoccupied with "good deals" online but they may be searching for a sense of control, a distraction from anxiety, and a feeling of mastery and competence, which may be absent in the real world that they live in. This may possibly explain the constant need to check for latest updates on a certain webpage and discomfort when faced with the inability to access those sites as and when one desires. It is almost, on some levels, like a trader needing to check on the positions he places in the trading market and the anxiety he faces when placed in a situation where access is compromised.

ONLINE PORNOGRAPHY ADDICTION

When we explore the genre of another potentially addictive online behaviour, Internet pornography addiction, it may be helpful to first look at the definitions for pornography addiction. Traditionally, pornography addiction is often considered as compulsive sexual activity with recurrent use of pornographic material, despite negative consequences to one's physical, mental, social, or financial well-being (Laier, Pawlikowski, Pekal, Schulte, & Brand, 2013).

With the advancement of technology, pornography addiction has evolved into various trajectories and may sometimes also refer to the use of Internet pornography that is problematic for an individual due to personal or social reasons, including excessive time spent viewing pornography instead of interacting with others (Twohig & Crosby, 2010). In other words, it refers to a situation where one's engagement with online pornographic materials has come to a point where it compromises self-care and social and occupational functioning. Individuals struggling with such issues may report a dip in mood states, social isolation, jeopardising a career, marked impairment in effectiveness and productivity, or financial consequences as a result of their excessive Internet pornography use.

When pornography finds extra leverage with technological advancements, the issue of compulsive pornography use seems more complicated than ever. The ease of access, the anonymity, the possibility of getting one's hands on any material related to almost every conceivable sexual fantasy becomes a huge and powerful draw of Internet pornography.

An interesting school of thought that draws parallels between drug addiction and pornography addiction suggests pornography addiction develops much like a drug addiction. After an initially rewarding experience with pornography, individuals may experience uncontrollable urges to obtain sexual satisfaction through that form of entertainment (Griffiths, 2001). Over time, the connection between Internet pornography and sexual gratification becomes positively reinforced, and the urges and cravings to engage in Internet pornography becomes increasingly strong, powerful and somewhat irresistible. It is almost like the brain is being rewired to believe that Internet pornography is the only way one can achieve certain degrees of sexual gratification.

Cues that used to be neutral, like turning on the computer, using the search option of a particular browser or simply sitting by the computer becomes strong triggers for engaging in Internet pornography. This appears to be extremely similar to drug users being triggered by seemingly neutral and irrelevant cues like a cubicle in the public toilet because that is the place they use to do drugs. It is also important to note that only a small group of people who have engaged in pornography or Internet pornography eventually become addicted and have extreme difficulty moving past Grohol's enchantment phase. One of the key features of the online behaviour, like most behavioural addictions, becoming problematic is when it causes impairment in one's life. Some examples include a student not leaving for school on time because he cannot tear himself away from engaging in Internet pornography at home, or a student not meeting his assignment deadlines because he could not stop himself from spending hours on pornographic websites while doing online research for his assignments.

In all these examples, the common denominator would be the impairment brought about by the behaviour and the inability to stop or moderate use despite negative consequences. The other key feature common to many people engaged in compulsive Internet pornography is the shame and guilt that accompanies the behaviour. Unfortunately some of them get entangled in the vicious cycle of firstly engaging in pornography to seek out positive or perhaps even euphoric experiences, feeling extremely guilty and shameful afterwards and then using pornography again to numb those unpleasant thoughts and feelings about their behaviours. This brings us to another feature which may be present in many caught in the web of behavioural addictions – the constant and repetitive use of a particular behaviour to escape reality or numb unpleasant emotions.

The other issue of concern with compulsive Internet pornography use is the possibility of experiencing tolerance. The term tolerance, in the genre of addiction, generally refers to the need to engage a certain behaviour with increasing frequency or intensity to achieve the desired effect or "high". This trait could be depicted simply by a steady increase in the time spent engaging in Internet pornography over time (usually to the detriment of the other aspects of one's life) or an increase in the intensity of the pornographic material accessed. Some examples may include rape fantasies, sadomasochistic pornography, child pornography and fetishes. Many clinicians have observed how prolonged and repetitive exposure to such materials can dramatically distort one's perception about human sexuality, resulting in the normalisation of abnormal sexual activities. This in turns affects interpersonal relationships and possibly sexual intimacy with their partners, leading to further isolation and the risk of increased compulsive sexual acting out to seek gratification that they cannot seem to derive from real relationships. The availability, the easy access and the anonymity of Internet pornography makes it easier for a person with unsatisfactory relationships to seek solace from it.

ONLINE GAMBLING ADDICTION

To date, gambling disorder is the only behavioural addiction to be officially classified as a diagnosable disorder in the *Diagnostic and Statistical Manual of Mental Disorders* (DSM-5). It is defined by the University of Maryland Medical Center (Vorvick, Linda, Merrill & Michelle, 2010) as the inability to resist impulses to gamble, which can lead to severe personal or social consequences. Individuals must meet at least four out of the nine following DSM-5 symptoms within a 12-month period. These symptoms include:

- A need to gamble with increasing amounts of money in order to achieve the desired excitement
- Restlessness or irritability when attempting to cut down or stop gambling
- Repeated unsuccessful efforts to control, cut down or stop gambling
- A preoccupation with gambling (e.g., having persistent thoughts of reliving past gambling experiences, handicapping or planning the next venture, thinking of ways to get money with which to gamble)
- A tendency to gamble when feeling distressed (e.g., helpless, guilty, anxious, depressed)
- A tendency to chase one's losses
- A tendency to lie in order to conceal the extent of involvement with gambling
- Jeopardising or losing a significant relationship, job, or educational or career opportunity because of gambling
- The reliance on others to provide money to relieve desperate financial situations caused by gambling

In terms of diagnosis, online gambling addiction is essentially diagnosed using the same criteria as "offline" or "conventional" gambling disorder. There are, however, several elements of Internet gambling that can potentially cause it to be more addictive than the typical type of gambling that goes on in a traditional gambling venue (e.g., turf clubs, casinos, lottery booths, underground gambling dens and slot machine clubs).

THE SECRECY BEHIND THE PROBLEM

When a gambler spends two or three days gambling at a regulated gambling venue, he may possibly be spotted by someone at some point (e.g., friends, co-workers, venue staff, family members). The online gamblers, on the other hand, can be sheltered within the comfort of the virtual cyberworld which promises a certain degree of anonymity (at least in the eyes and mind of the gambler). With this added online feature, one can now gamble at work, at home, or even on smartphones without anyone really being aware that they are actually gambling.

THE RISK OF DEVELOPING TRAITS LIKE CHASING LOSSES AND TOLERANCE

Online gambling puts players in a position where the access to money (be it via a credit card or a virtual paying account) is easily accessible. This setup obviously increases the likelihood of one becoming more impulsive than usual, resulting in the plausibility of placing higher stakes and chasing losses in a bigger way as compared to gambling in more traditional settings. It can sometimes become disturbingly easy for online users to forget that electronic money is still real money, resulting in users spending more than what they can realistically afford. In some countries, social safeguards are in place with ATM machines located on different levels from the casino, in order to reduce accessibility to cash. The relatively easy access to money in online gambling plants the seeds for the development of traits like a higher tolerance and tendency to chase losses, two criteria of gambling disorder in DSM-5.

THE DECEPTION OF TRIAL GAMES

One of the shady tactics used by some online gambling sites (particularly those that are not regulated by social safeguard policies) is to offer a trial version of their games. The objective is to increase the comfort level of new players, creating the perception that they are dealing with something safe and winnable. To put it simply, the odds of winning in the trial games are inflated artificially in the player's favour, causing them to buy in to the idea that the successes they had and "money" they won in the trial game is a direct representation of the kind of success they are likely to achieve when they risk real money. Clearly, the moment the trial games end and real games begin, the house always has the advantage.

THE DIFFICULTY IN PRACTISING AVOIDANCE STRATEGIES

A very basic component of conventional addiction treatment is the avoidance of places that may potentially trigger the urge to engage in addictive behaviours. For someone with a gambling problem, the first few places on this list would probably be the gambling venues: neighbourhood lottery booths, casinos, clubs with slot machines where there are plenty of opportunities to gamble. With online gambling made readily available, using this particular strategy to avoid temptation becomes a whole lot more challenging. Every computer or smartphone with Internet access (home, work or even on the move) becomes a virtual gambling venue with a hard-to-ignore presence.

THE DIFFICULTY IN IMPLEMENTING SOCIAL AND PERSONAL SAFEGUARDS

With a number of social safeguards available for different settings, a gambler may be denied entry from a gambling venue of choice (e.g., casino exclusions) for a stipulated period of time if a problem is identified. On an individual level, if a gambler finds visiting overseas gambling venues or gambling cruises an issue, there could be arrangements made for safekeeping of the passport by a trusted person (e.g., a family member). There is, however, little to prevent a compulsive gambler from accessing online gambling sites at will. The current regulatory systems for online gambling is somewhat lacking worldwide, resulting in many sites not having policies on temporarily or permanently restricting access for a special sub-population (e.g., for the underaged, the financially compromised, the compulsive gambler) that should clearly not be gambling.

Aside from the operational diagnostic criteria for gambling disorder, one important factor to consider in a preliminary screen for the existence of gambling problems would be whether the gambler is gambling in way that is harmful to himself and those around him (in the form of social and occupational malfunction, incurrence of debts, draining out the finances of family members, creating anxiety and distress for people around him, etc.); or if the gambler is gambling with money he cannot afford to lose. Once the line is crossed, it is often safe to assume that the person in question is, at the very least, struggling with problem gambling.

For those who are struggling with either offline or online gambling addiction, it almost seems like they have developed a disordered or pathological relationship with gambling evidenced by the fact that once they start, they almost always have problems controlling, moderating or stopping at will and with time, the behaviour usually spirals out of control.

There are many interesting similarities between online gambling and other online compulsive behaviours in the sense that many people actually engage in those behaviours on a moderate level without marked impairments in their lives. One of the factors, however, that makes gambling distinct from other online behavioural addictions is the difficulty (especially for those who have met the criteria for gambling disorder) of "turning back the clock"; of getting gamblers who have crossed the line to go back on a pathway of safe, responsible and recreational gambling.

CASE STUDY

Robert is a 40-year-old housing agent who has been gambling recreationally since the age of 16. It started with private bets on soccer matches, pool games and cards. By the time he was 20, he was gambling regularly on horses, the lottery and onboard cruise ships. Although the time and money spent on his gambling has steadily increased over the years, Robert has somewhat managed to keep his gambling within affordable limits. At the age of 35, some friends introduced him to an online soccer betting site and some illegal bookies. With online betting, he found himself losing the previous control he had on his gambling behaviour. He no longer set limits and would often be gambling with more and more money per stake to chase his losses. Along with online soccer betting, he started experimenting with online casinos. Gradually he chalked up more debts and got increasingly isolated from his family. During outings with his wife and children, he would often be visiting the washroom, checking the latest football scores and having a go at the Internet casino table games or slot machines via his smartphone. As Robert lost track of the money he spent on gambling online and assumed that he probably won more than he had lost, he was shocked when he received his latest credit card statement. He had, in a short period of three months, accumulated a five-figure debt.

PREVENTION STRATEGIES

One of the helpful things to be mindful about – and mentioned a few times earlier in this chapter – is the difference between healthy and recreational engagement in online activities and maladaptive preoccupation. There are some simple but important questions to ask to determine the likelihood of the existence of a problem. These questions include:

- Has the online behaviour affected the ability to perform and function in other important aspects of life? Are the roles of a student, an employee/employer, a father/mother, partner, a co-worker, etc. performed?

- Are these online behaviours sought out as the only means to comfort and soothe unpleasant emotions?
- Is reality consistently escaped (to a point where it creates problems in one's life) via the engagement of these behaviours?
- Are online relationships preferred and replacing most real-life relationships?
- Is there a marked decline in self-care (e.g., hygiene levels, health) as a result of the engagement in the online activity?
- Has engaging in or thinking about the online activity taken centre stage, causing a loss in interest in previously-enjoyed activities?

If the answer is positive to any one of the above questions, there is a high likelihood that the person is experiencing some problems as a result of online behaviour. Taking Grohol's model as a reference, there would then be some steps that can be taken to move from the stage of enchantment to the stage of moderation – from problematic, excessive engagement to healthy, moderated use:

- The recognition and the willingness to admit the existence of a problem is an important first step. This could be a stepping stone to make self-directed adjustments around an online activity, seek professional help or talk to a trusted someone about the issue.

- Get involved in a hobby or an interest that doesn't involve the Internet, smartphones, computers or portable devices. This strategy has proven to be helpful in almost all kinds of addictive behaviours. With time off from an activity that used to take up inordinate amounts of time, a void is left. Hence, it is important to be able to fill up this void with meaningful activities.

- Draw a clear line between what one needs to do and likes to do. In short, this is about setting priorities and time management. This strategy proposes that a person put aside time and fulfill important commitments in the occupational, social and personal aspect of one's life before engaging in pleasurable or recreational online activities.

- Form real and meaningful relationships with people. If one has been detached from a group of friends as a result of excessive engagement in online activities, it is helpful to attempt to rebuild those relationships. Proactively calling someone up, arranging for a group outing or even meeting up with a colleague for tea are some ways one could attempt to reconnect with people again. Our brain operates most optimally when we connect and form relationships with others. Science has shown that social connections, interactions and transactions change the neural activities in one's brain, resulting in a reduction of stress, anxiety and depressive symptoms and an enhancement of calm and happy feelings.

- Seek professional help. If there are tremendous difficulties regulating Internet use, the person should speak to professionals such as those at the Institute of Mental Health's National Addictions Management Service (NAMS) and at TOUCH Community Services.

LEGAL AND FORENSIC IMPLICATIONS OF INTERNET ADDICTION

Dr Jaydip Sarkar

Internet addiction is increasingly becoming a worldwide problem and young people are particularly affected by it. The addiction can critically affect young lives, with major legal and forensic implications. This chapter looks at how Internet addiction by young people can lead to crime with major consequences for the users, their families and larger society.

COMMON CYBERCRIMES

Common criminal activities over the Internet include:

Offence Type	Victimisation	Perpetration
Stalking	Cyber bullying, stalking	Harassment
Security Breach	Piracy and breach of copyright laws	Illegal downloading, hacking information
Sexual	Sexting, sexual violence	Online grooming, rape, assault, upskirt photography, child pornography

Offence Type	Victimisation	Perpetration
Fraud	Credit card fraud, identity theft	Financial scams, online gambling, love scams
Others	Religious and racial abuse	Drug trafficking, violence, terrorism

NATURE OF ONLINE CRIMINAL ACTIVITIES

- Illegal downloading – Downloading film, music or video clips without permission is a common illegal activity that adolescents carry out on the Internet. In a survey of 559 young people of age 10 to 24, 57.4% of the participants admitted that they had downloaded film or music without obtaining permission from the license holders.

- Cheating behaviour – It is easy to cheat others online because you are anonymous to others and your identity can be hidden easily if you wish.

- Unlicensed online gambling – Online gambling can include poker, live casinos, sports betting, lotteries, and bingo. A new remote gambling law was passed in October 2014 to clamp down on unregulated online betting. Unlicensed gambling websites have since been blocked and it is illegal to gamble on these portals.

- Credit card fraud – Credit cards are now the preferred mode of online payment for many transactions. Unfortunately the plethora of such transactions has created various credit card offences. The financial burden due to such fraudulent use falls upon the issuers, the banking industry and credit card holders. As a result, you and me, i.e., the community, bears the brunt of such offences.

IMPACT OF CRIMINAL BEHAVIOUR

Pathological Internet use can lead to criminal behaviour, with significant psychosocial impairment to:

- the person – loss of interest in alternative pleasures, isolation, relationship discord, academic failure, financial debt, job loss and prison sentences.
- the public – as primary victims where there is sexual, financial, racial and religiously abusive harm caused or where there has been a breach in security and privacy (of individuals or organisations); or as secondary victims in the form of family members suffering from the consequences of the actions of the perpetrator.
- the government – the cost incurred to prosecute lawbreakers, extra policing, monitoring and surveillance via CCTVs, crime reduction policies, etc.
- the society – loss of a productive member of society to this habit and if convicted (which means a prison term), a break-up of families and communities.

YOUNG PERSONS AS PERPETRATORS

The following case studies illustrate some of the major crimes that young persons commit over the Internet.

....

CASE STUDY: HACKING

John is a 17-year-old boy with excellent programming skills. He spends long periods of time locked away in his bedroom with his computer. He is bright and does well in his studies. His parents are really pleased with him as he is far superior to his younger brother in terms of educational achievements, discipline and obedience and has never caused any problems. His mother was ill with depression when John was a child and he spent a lot of time on his own, playing alone. During the year-end school vacation John became interested in computer security and discovered certain flaws in a well-known operating system. He managed to hack (deliberately obtain unauthorised access to computers or their contents) into four foreign sites without being detected by their system administrators. Earlier he had acquired a cable network's high-speed link to download files from the Internet. Emboldened by his success in hacking into the four sites, he carried on his further exploration and eventually found a way to access the server. Once he had gained access, he amended several files and configured a backdoor entry so that in future he could access the server without having to hack into it. No tangible damage was caused to the computer systems of the companies and servers that he had used illegally.

In his sentencing, the judge said there was criminal intent and even though there was no tangible damage, societal harm had been caused. The anti-social conduct by the youth undermined public and international confidence in the integrity and viability of computers and compromised Singapore's efforts to position itself as a global e-commerce hub. It would also negatively impact foreign companies' confidence in investing within Singapore. The judge said in his closing statement that he hoped John's "intelligence, talent and potential" will be used to bring "immense value" to the country, and felt that the experience in prison will "instil a sense of maturity and responsibility in him for using his vast knowledge in legitimate ways".

CASE STUDY: SEXUAL OFFENCES

Victor is a 15-year-old boy whose mother abandoned him when he was a baby. He was cared for by his paternal grandmother, and when she died, Victor was looked after by his alcoholic father, a taxi driver. Although Victor was a bright student, his father was never satisfied with his performance. Victor was subjected to severe physical punishment and kept in isolation which made him very fearful of his father. After moving to secondary school, he found it hard to cope with academic pressures and quickly found a peer group with whom he started smoking and visiting websites that he was unaware of until then. He found and watched online pornographic videos. He was afraid at first of his father finding out, but watching porn and masturbating afterwards led to a sense of relief from an oppressive and indifferent family home while giving him a sense of pleasure.

Soon he was pretending to be an adult and had become a member of adult porn websites, assuming the online name of Dick, a reflection of his preoccupation with sex and masturbation. While chatting with older males he was offered money for uploading exciting real life sexual material in lieu of free access to more hardcore material on some websites. They were looking for boy-on-boy sexual material. Victor befriended a younger student at school, whom he had taken a liking to. This boy was slightly intellectually disabled and was also lonely. Victor acted as his protector from his bullies. Shortly after, he taught the young boy, who was 12, how to masturbate and engaged in mutual masturbation. At one point, he offered him money if he performed oral sex on Victor. Victor recorded this incident, which took place in a public place, and uploaded it to the website. While checking his laptop, Victor's aunt found out about his illegal online activities and informed the police. Subsequent investigation led to the exposure of a large syndicate of paedophiles who were using children like Victor for their pleasure and gratification. Victor was charged and sentenced to the Singapore Boys' Home for sexual offences.

CASE STUDY: CREDIT CARD FRAUD

Chong, a big-sized 16-year-old boy, was travelling with his family to the United States on holiday. The family was in transit at the airport in Hamburg for a few hours. Unbeknownst to his parents, Chong had found a credit card on the seat next to him during the flight from Singapore to Hamburg. He took and hid it in his clothing. As he was a mature 16-year-old, his parents had faith in him and allowed him to shop on his own. He made several unauthorised purchases using the credit card he found while in transit. He ran up bills of several thousand dollars as he bought gold rings and wrist watches – small items which he could hide in his luggage without drawing undue notice from his parents. His desire was to give a ring to his girlfriend and wear the expensive watch in school to impress everyone. He was eventually caught and penalised.

CASE STUDY: WOUNDING RELIGIOUS FEELINGS

In a high-profile case following the demise of Singapore's first Prime Minister, a young boy was charged for wounding religious feelings of followers of one religion and for distributing obscene material. He had uploaded homemade videos on YouTube where he expressed his personal opinions and views that were considered by the judiciary to have both hurt religious feelings as well as corrupted the minds of others. He spent several months in prison on remand and was convicted of the charges. The 16-year-old claimed he had simply exercised his freedom of speech, a constitutional right. Dismissing his appeal against the conviction and sentence, the presiding judge said the teenager had engaged in activities that "were done in the noble disguise of freedom of speech" but that his "deliberate use of vulgarities and crude language to provoke reactions seems like someone throwing stones at the windows of a neighbour's house to force them to notice him and force them to come out to quarrel or fight. This doesn't sound like freedom of speech at all." The honorable judge further noted that the youngster was "obviously not a person without talent. He has a command of the English language which could be put to good use", adding that "real debate and rational discussions of social issues can flourish in an environment of goodwill and civil language".

YOUNG PERSONS AS VICTIMS

On the other hand, young people may often be victimised by others online who are quite adept in identifying their emotional vulnerabilities based upon what they say about themselves, the kind of photographs and material they upload, and the keenness with which they tend to believe, associate with or befriend relative strangers on the Internet. They tend to be naïve, unusually trusting of others, gullible, submissive, friendless and may also have intellectual disabilities in some instances. They are often young people who are looking for a father figure. On the other extreme are those who are sensation-seeking, rebellious and impulsive. They are keen to experience the "fun" of an adult life precociously. Research has found that girls aged 13 to 17 are most at risk as victims.

CYBER BULLYING

Cyber bullying includes sending nasty text messages or emails, or setting up a hate group on a social networking site. The bullying may happen 24 hours a day, every day, and victims are often targeted even when they are in the comfort of their own homes. Images and text messages can be circulated very quickly and widely on the Internet, which makes it very hard to combat cyberbullying. Being a victim of cyberbullying can be very distressing for a young person as most of the time they do not know who is bullying them and why.

SEXTING

The term "sexting" is a word-mix of sex and texting. It involves the use of technology to share personal sexual content. Other terms for it that parents and teachers may hear are "cybersexing", or "doxing". The content can vary from sexually explicit text messages to images of partial nudity to sexual images or video. This content is usually created to be sent to a partner or between groups. Photos and videos are often created via webcam or smartphone camera, and are shared on social networking sites such as Facebook, Twitter, Tumblr, Flickr and video sites such as YouTube. If a young person under the age of 18 engages in sexting by creating, distributing or possessing an explicit photo or video of him- or herself, this will potentially constitute a case of child abuse.

SEXUAL ABUSE AND GROOMING

Online grooming is the process by which an adult with an inappropriate sexual interest in children will approach a child online, with the intention of developing a relationship with that child, then to meet them in person and intentionally cause harm.

CASE STUDY

Sheena, a 16-year-old girl, met Mr Tan online, a married journalist in his mid-thirties and a mentor for young people through an online mentoring programme that a newspaper runs in Singapore. Initially the quality of her engagement and involvement with him centred on various international and national issues, such as politics, history and international affairs. He said he was trying to understand the people he mentored, which meant he would ask various questions about the person's personal life in order to represent the individual better in his reports. Sheena had problems at home with her family and was going through spells of sadness and crying. Thinking that Mr Tan could help her, she confided about being bullied at school and that her father would beat her. This "struck a chord" with Mr Tan who said he too had undergone such experiences, immediately making Sheena feel close to him. She told him she had consulted a psychiatrist, was missing school and her grades were falling.

Mr Tan said he felt empathy towards her and wanted to support her more. They started meeting at various places for lunch or movies. He knew he should not be engaging with a mentee in this personal manner and so took precautions in terms of where they met. After meeting him a few times, Sheena felt relaxed and less depressed, telling him that being with him made her feel good. At some stage they started hugging and kissing and it culminated in the two having sexual intercourse on few occasions. He told Sheena that he was married but lied that he and his wife had an "open relationship" which meant he was allowed to have sex with others. After a few months, as Sheena became more emotionally dependent on him and when she wanted to spend more time with him, he tried to end their relationship. Sheena became suicidal and took an overdose of Panadol tablets as well as cut her wrist. In hospital she confided to her mother the real reason for her suicidal behaviour. The parents lodged a police complaint and Mr Tan was arrested for sexual penetration of a minor, a serious sexual offence and tried in court, where he said that whilst he knew sexual activity with a minor was illegal, Sheena was doing so consensually. All of Sheena's personal history and family situation was discussed and debated in an open court, much to her humiliation and further emotional upset.

FINANCIAL AND LOVE SCAM

CASE STUDY

Linda aged 17, met Tony, who claimed to be 21, on Yahoo chat rooms. He seemed very interested and keen to meet her. He was working reportedly for a multi-national company in Jakarta, earning a good salary. She found him to be "assertive, authoritative, hard-working and successful" online and although she tried to meet him in person, he was never available due to his supposedly busy work schedule. Tony had bowled her over by saying things that made her feel he was a "good mentor who could possibly be my guide as my parents were busy with their own lives and I was quite lonely as the only child". She even decided to marry him in her mind within weeks of meeting him online despite not having met him. As a daughter of wealthy parents, Linda would get substantial pocket money. Her parents would also give her money if she asked for it without necessarily checking how it was spent. Tony started to ask to borrow money from her, each time in larger amounts. The reasons for his borrowings ranged from lack of adequate allowance payment by his company, to delay in his salary coming through, to having to support himself doing two jobs. He reportedly made her jealous and insecure by saying he would borrow from another woman when she questioned him about his borrowing. She said on other occasions "he would make me feel guilty, threaten to leave me, start crying on the phone or not talk to me for several days".

He then started asking her about her bank account details, saying one of his friends abroad wanted to send him some money but due to international laws, he could not send the money to Indonesia directly and whether she could accept the funds and then forward them to his account. She did not know what to do and asked for some time to think about it. She never doubted his word, her only concern being whether this was legal or not.

She was therefore shocked one day to find the police at her doorstep. They had traced her computer IP address from the computer recovered from "Tony" (not his real name) who had earlier been arrested for being the mastermind of a global money laundering scam wherein innocent victims would be lured into a trap. Their accounts would be used to divert illegally obtained funds from one country to another. Some would be offered monetary gains while others did it out of "love". The perpetrators lived and operated from different countries who identified vulnerable and lonely girls and women, then offered them counselling, friendship, and availability through a virtual relationship. Once the perpetrators gained the trust of their victims, the rest was easy to achieve. Linda was lucky that she escaped with only the loss of a few thousand dollars as some other victims ended up with prison sentences for allowing the use of their bank accounts for money laundering purposes.

REASONS FOR LAWBREAKING BEHAVIOUR

A child or young person whose real needs are not being met in the real world engages in activities online that are designed to meet those needs in the virtual world.

INDIVIDUAL REASONS

Many young people who engage in such activities are trying to escape from the stresses of everyday life. In many cases this kind of compulsive behaviour is associated with underlying states of tension and agitation which are relieved through the completion of the act. The reduction in underlying emotional pain and tension leads to greater use of the Internet as a stress-relieving mechanism. In such instances, their use of the computer is less about using it as an information tool, and more about finding a psychological escape to cope with life's problems.

For some others, there is antisocial thinking, lack of compassion and concern about the feelings and safety of others as well as frank mental disorders that are implicated in the offense. There are certain factors which put young people at higher risk of perpetrating sexual offences. These can be adapted for those who engage in non-sexual offences online.

- Distorted sexual scripts – The first and foremost reason is deviant sexual arousal. The potential offender somehow gets "programmed" due to personal life experiences to be sexually aroused in perverse ways. They have fantasies of carrying out deviant acts and often improve upon their modus operandi with successive acts.

- Intimacy deficits – A second factor is the inability to emotionally connect and socialise with the opposite gender and a lack of appropriate and satisfying adult sexual relationships. This is also known as "impersonal sex" where women, their body parts or their accessories are seen as sexual "objects" and used for arousal and masturbation. These people are often isolated, loners, socially inadequate, cold and impersonal. They may spend long hours on the Internet or on their phones, gaming, texting, or engaging in deviant pleasures.

- Antisocial thinking – A third factor is lack of empathy or compassion for others, leading to breaking social and legal rules, hoping to get away with it or taking sufficient prior care so that they are not caught. Many such individuals are antisocial in their attitudes and lifestyles.
- Emotional dysregulation – A fourth factor is the use of sex, drugs, gambling, online sexual offences, etc. as ways to deal with underlying emotional problems with controlling anger, understanding their feelings, impulsivity and personal distress. Stress, drugs or alcohol often act as disinhibiting factors, allowing them to do what they may have only been thinking about.
- Other factors: Very rarely do people have a major mental disorder or significant intellectual impairments that affect their judgments so significantly that they commit such acts.

FAMILIAL REASONS

In a survey, 56% of teens said that their parents know some of what they do online, but not everything. A quarter of those surveyed report that their parents do not have time to check on what they do online. Broad reasons for deviant activities may include broken families where there is either little or no communication or harsh parenting styles. Forcing children to become immersed in a strict routine of school work without social activities and playtime with peers could be potentially harmful. Such a regime does not allow children to learn ways to either emotionally connect or engage in pro-social pleasurable activities with others. This creates loners who tend to find pleasures (and relief from stress) on their own, often in pathological ways. These young people can become susceptible to addictive behaviours, using it as a way of escape from real life stress, to cope with their emotional and social isolation. Hence, parents should help to create a balance of personal and social as well as academic and leisure activities for their children.

ENVIRONMENTAL OR SOCIETAL REASONS

Internet use and online crimes are a new phenomenon, having only emerged in the past two decades. So why is it that seemingly well-behaved children from reasonably settled familial backgrounds become criminals when they are online? Clinical research suggests that cyberspace can act as an enabler of crime. In the main, two factors are implicated:

- the anonymity of being on the Internet within the comforts of operating from one's own home
- the convenience of engaging in inappropriate communication and applications

First, online experiences often occur in the privacy of one's bedroom, giving the perception that online use of the Internet is personal and untraceable. This false sense of anonymity facilitates much more open and frank communication with other users since there is decreased ability to physically observe signs of insincerity, disapproval, or judgment in facial expression, as would be typical in face-to-face interactions. Consequently, users become disinhibited which allows them to play out hidden criminal or repressed sexual fantasies in a private "lab", which is what the bedroom often becomes for the young person. They come across like-minded individuals as well as those that prey on young minds and vulnerabilities. They are more likely to experiment online – in terms of sexual, fraudulent and other criminal activities, as users feel encouraged and validated by the acceptance of the cyberspace culture. By hiding behind the anonymity of the computer screen, they feel less accountable for their actions online.

Second, the convenience of interactive online applications such as email, chat rooms, online forums and personal messaging services, or indeed role-playing games and forums provide a vehicle to meet others. The proliferation of special interest rooms, groups, and games contributes to easy access for a curious person's initial exploration, whatever the area of interest: relationships and sex, acquisition and fraud, or hostile and intimidatory crime. However, the curious person may be completely unprepared for what they are getting into initially. Titles such as the "Dominance and Submission Room", the "Fetish Room", or the "Bisexual Room" may intrigue a casual browser who is initially shocked, but at the same time titillated by the permissiveness of others engaged in virtual sex. Such virtual environments are more seductive than most people anticipate and may lead down a path that may end in addiction and offence (see next section on Process).

PROCESS OF "DESENSITISATION" LEADING TO OFFENCE

Online behaviour of a deviant nature follows a certain set

of stages which culminates in offending behaviour. It is not that the young person is a career criminal or has an antisocial personality, but that the enabling nature of cyberspace in conjunction with personal and social circumstances creates a process that ends in an offence. Users start off as normal persons who progress gradually into deviant fantasies and behaviours such that topics and interests that they normally find reprehensible become acceptable, and after continued use they become "desensitised" to the experience. This is the process of "addiction" except that in this addiction there are two victims: the primary victim and the perpetrator himself (and his family) as secondary victim/s.

1. Stage of Discovery: In this stage, a young boy doing research online for a school project may accidentally obtain access to a pornography website or a girl enters a social chat room and meets an adult male posing as a boy who entices her to have cybersex with him. In either case, the person discovers the sexual thrill of the act, which opens the door for further exploration.

2. Stage of Experimentation: Encouraged by the anonymity of electronic transactions, an online user will secretly explore and experiment without the fear of being caught. In this stage, a user tries out different chat rooms or chats with particular persons online, or indeed visits certain websites which are the most exciting and relevant to his or her area/s of interest. The user learns the inner workings of the chatroom, the nature of the relationship with the online friend, or accesses restricted material of a website that will

provide him the best virtual experience. In this stage, users believe that they can control their urges and deal with their virtual experimentation on their own terms.

3. Stage of Habituation: In this stage, the online user becomes bored with routine of what he does. He may engage in bolder chat fantasies, deeper conversations and greater exploration looking for a bigger thrill. The online experience heightens as the user engages in more adventurous, daring, and even deviant themes that may be sexual, fraudulent or revolve around security or intimidation. The user's activities thus take on riskier and riskier forms once he no longer derives the same thrill or pleasure from existing ones.

4. Stage of Compulsivity: In this stage, life becomes unmanageable as relationships or careers are jeopardised. The person spends longer periods of time searching for new material online and there is a possibility of him translating his actions from the virtual to the real world. For example, cybersex is no longer a virtual act but a sexual act that must be completed. The experience that commenced as relief from pain and anxiety, the reward for success, and a way to avoid addressing other emotional issues in the person's life, now becomes an obsession. The resultant compulsive behaviour can be akin to an altered state of consciousness in which normal sexual behaviour pales by comparison in terms of excitement.

5. Stage of Hopelessness: The person hits rock bottom once he realises the extent of damage done because of addiction. Feelings of hopelessness and helplessness develop. In this

stage, users may cancel their Internet service, disconnect modems, or install filtering software in the attempt to stop the compulsive behaviour. Since relapse is only a mouse click away, they may relapse back into old patterns beginning the cycle once again. In the hopeless stage, negative thinking about oneself, making such self-statements as: "I am helpless because I can't control my use", "I am weak", "I am defective", "I am worthless or disgusting because of my dirty habit", "Everything I do is wrong", "I am a failure". In this stage the user may seek professional help, confide in a person or become so reckless as though he seemingly wishes to be caught and punished for his actions, which by now he begins to loathe. Not everybody reaches this stage however.

RELEVANT LAWS IN SINGAPORE

Some of the common laws relevant for cybercrimes in Singapore are:

- Computer Misuse Act (CMA)
- Undesirable Publication Act 1998
- Wounding Religious Feeling (Section 292(1)(a) of Penal Code)
- Obscene act (Section 298 of Penal Code)
- Protection from Harassment Act
- Relevant Offences of a sexual nature are defined in the Penal Code, and include:
  - s354 – Assault or use of criminal force to a person with intent to outrage modesty

- s354A – Outraging modesty in certain circumstances
- s375 – Rape
- s376 – Sexual assault by penetration
- s376A – Sexual penetration of a minor under 16 years
- s376B – Commercial sex with a minor under 18 years
- s376E - Sexual grooming of a minor (amendment made in 2007)
- s376G – Incest
- s377A – Outrages on Decency
- Children and Young Persons Act (Cap 38) offence
  - s7 – Sexual Exploitation of child or young person

Most cybercrimes in Singapore are covered by the CMA. This legislation has "extra-territorial" effect. This means that for offences under this Act, the effect of the law will reach the offender, whatever his nationality or citizenship, outside as well as within Singapore. So even if an act has been committed by a person in any place outside Singapore, he may be dealt with as if the offence has been committed within Singapore. The section above, "Case Study: Credit Card Fraud" is a case in point.

HOW YOUNG PEOPLE CAN BE HELPED
HOW PARENTS CAN GUIDE THEIR CHILDREN

- Children can become responsible, ethical digital citizens with healthy online relationships. The same successful parenting skills that most parents use at home are the very tools to safeguard children. For parents with children who are more deviant and disruptive, a firmer approach with limit setting would be necessary.

- Strong relationships with children, setting up clear boundaries and consistent use of consequences for negative behaviours will help children perceive the parents as being fair and balanced. Words of affirmation, praise, receiving gifts, quality time, physical touch and parental love will help the child to feel connected.

- Parents can gain children's trust and encourage them to talk about any difficulties at school and/or with peers.

- Understanding the emotional and social development of children at different stages will aid parents' adaptability and acceptance of their child's developmental needs in a digital world.

UNDERSTANDING THE DIGITAL WORLD AND SUPERVISING COMPUTER USAGE

- Parents should understand the digital world children inhabit, by knowing how to operate and what kind of activities are possible on iPads, instant messaging, chats, computer games, game consoles, cell phones, text messaging, webcams, etc. Rather than ban the use of such devices which may make children more deceptive, engaging with them and finding out more will work better. In particular, parents should find out about various online digital games and what children are involved in.

- Teach children skills using the principle of 3Cs of responsible and resilient digital use: appropriate Contact, appropriate Content, and appropriate Conduct.
- Place computer systems in common areas where parents can see what children are doing rather than allow them to disappear into their bedrooms and out of sight.
- Monitor online friends and purchases.
- Set up parental controls through the use of appropriate parental control apps. More teens are accessing pornography via mobile phones due to lack of filters for these devices.

DEVELOPING CHILDREN HOLISTICALLY

- Encourage outdoor activities.
- Help develop social and interpersonal connections.
- Learn about the child's personal and school or college environments so that the child is less likely to seek online contacts as ways of dealing with stress and isolation.

ADDRESSING A CHILD'S NEEDS

Beyond what a responsible parent can do, there are other issues that may require help from other individuals and professionals. Many young people may suffer from mental health problems that require professional help. Adults need to provide reasonable control, discipline, care and guidance. Chaotic, uncommunicative, and harsh parenting styles tend to drive young people into the cyberworld. Similarly, a disturbance in school-based peer (or teacher) relationships can act as a factor that promotes online abuse.

PROFESSIONAL HELP

Some common issues that require professional intervention are:

- Mental health problems: Attention Deficit Hyperactivity Disorder, Autism Spectrum Disorder, Depressive and Anxiety disorder, Conduct Disorder and Other Addictions.
- Family problems: Sibling conflicts, marital problems between parents leading to parent-child conflicts.
- School problems: Academic failure, bullying, social isolation, low motivation or morale.

LEGAL HELP

MINISTRY OF SOCIAL AND FAMILY DEVELOPMENT (MSF)

This is the statutory agency tasked to provide a range of family and child services across Singapore. Service directory link: http://app.msf.gov.sg/dfcs/familyservice/default.aspx

The Rehabilitation and Protection Group provides probation services as well as a range of other services:

- Adult Protective Service
- Child Protective Service
- Clinical and Forensic Psychology Service
- Operations and Service Capability Branch
- Youth Residential Service

Link: http://app.msf.gov.sg/About-MSF/Our-People/ Divisions-at-MSF/Social-Development-and-Support/ Rehabilitation-and-Protection-Group/Probation-Service

FAMILY JUSTICE COURTS OF SINGAPORE

There are family service centres providing a range of legal and statutory services that can be accessed through the link: https://www.familyjusticecourts.gov.sg/Pages/default.aspx

FORENSIC REHABILITATION, INTERVENTION, EVALUATION & NETWORK DEVELOPMENT SERVICES (FRIENDS)

The Child Guidance Clinic at the Institute of Mental Health provides comprehensive and integrated multi-disciplinary assessment and intervention services for the following groups facing mental health issues:

- Young offenders
- Youth-at-risk of committing offences
- Victims of child abuse
- Children and parents involved in complex custody and access disputes

Details of the service are available at: https://www.imh.com.sg/clinical/page.aspx?id=262

HELP FOR SCHOOL AND FAMILY BASED ISSUES

School counsellors as well as services within Departments of Child and Adolescent Psychiatry, Institute of Mental Health and other restructured hospitals, and Family Service Centres can be accessed for school-related difficulties.

HELP FOR CYBER ADDICTION PROBLEMS

There are various services to help individuals better cope with Internet use. Refer to the next chapter of this book to find more information and contact details.

INTERVENTION: TREATING INTERNET AND GAMING ADDICTIONS

Dr Choo Hyekyung
Chong Ee Jay

As discussed in the previous chapters, whether or not Internet addiction is a clinical disorder is still debatable amongst researchers and clinicians. However, it is undeniable that there exist children and parents who suffer from the negative consequences of excessive Internet use.

When one is diagnosed with Internet or gaming addiction, there is damage to daily functioning in the areas of school, work and social relationships. Typical complaints made by parents of children who play video games or use the Internet excessively include poor school performance, strained parent-child relationships, social isolation and neglected basic needs, such as sleeping, eating, and personal hygiene. As the child appears to be getting addicted to the Internet or gaming, the parents become desperate to control the child's usage. Often, parents try various means to control the child's computer usage, ranging from setting limits to confiscating the computer and modem, or even physically punishing the child, but to no avail in most cases. Most of these means only leave parents feeling frustrated and helpless.

Despite the impairments caused by addiction to the Internet or gaming, few children or their parents seek professional help. Data from our local study, which identified 8.7% of 2,998 youth in Singapore as pathological online gamers (Choo et al., 2010), have shown that only 10.8% of the identified pathological gamers reported to have sought professional help for their gaming addiction (Choo, 2012). The low rate of seeking professional help can be explained by various reasons, but probably best by the fact that most children and their parents do not know what kind of professional help is available, how it works, and where to get such help.

This chapter provides an overview of intervention models employed to treat Internet and gaming addictions, introduces some helpful components of potentially effective interventions, along with one local example of a community-based intervention programme, and discusses the agenda for further development of intervention models. As the fundamentals of intervention are similar between online gaming addiction and other types of Internet-related addiction, this chapter will refer to both Internet and gaming addictions as the focus of these three intervention models.

INTERVENTION MODELS FOR INTERNET AND GAMING ADDICTIONS

Research literature and news media report various intervention models for Internet and gaming addictions that are useful to youths and adults.

In Singapore, however, there is a limited variety of intervention models implemented for Internet and gaming addictions. Among the three main intervention models to be introduced below, the first two – cognitive behavioural therapy and family therapy – are rarely implemented at the community level in Singapore. The third one – multi-dimensional counselling – is deemed the most common mode of intervention for Internet and gaming addictions. Despite the limited use of cognitive behavioural therapy and family therapy as treatment models for Internet and gaming addictions in the community, the two therapies will be introduced in detail because multi-dimensional counselling incorporates key elements of the former two treatments that have the most available empirical evidence for effectiveness.

COGNITIVE BEHAVIOURAL THERAPY

Cognitive Behavioural Therapy (CBT) is probably the most well-known psychotherapy approach found to be effective in treating many mental disorders including addictions. The underlying notion for CBT is that a person's behaviours and emotions are guided and shaped by his or her thoughts and beliefs, and the accompanying dysfunctional behaviours and emotional distress are a result of distorted thoughts and belief systems. Accordingly, CBT aims to change the client's distorted and erroneous thought patterns into more functional, realistic, and logical ones in order to achieve the desired emotional and behavioural changes. In addition, as reflected in the term "behavioural", CBT corrects dysfunctional behavioural patterns using behavioural modification techniques while working on cognitive restructuring. CBT is a highly structured and directive therapeutic approach, focusing on the "here and now".

For cognitive behavioural therapists, Internet addiction is understood as a maladaptive coping behaviour affected by distorted cognitions about oneself and the world (Abreu & Góes, 2011). For example, a 14-year-old boy may develop dependency on the Internet as a substitute behaviour to cope with deficiency in his social relationships, the latter resulting from an overgeneralised perception or belief that there is no social and family support for him (Davis, 2001). CBT would then help him identify:

- Situations triggering the desire to use the Internet (e.g., coming back after school to find nobody around at home)
- Associated maladaptive thoughts (e.g., "No one, not even my own parents, cares about me in the real world, but only my virtual friends do.")
- Feelings following the thoughts (e.g., feeling lonely and rejected in the real world as well as excited about interacting with virtual friends online)
- How the triggering situation, maladaptive thoughts and feelings are linked to cause the prolonged, excessive use of the Internet

Through the cognitive-behavioural approach, the client is guided to replace his maladaptive thought with a more realistic one. For example, instead of the overgeneralised notion that no one cares about him, the boy could be advised to objectively evaluate the reality that in fact, some people, including his parents and a few close friends of his from his childhood, do care about him, that the reason for the absence of parents at home after school is not because they do not care about him but because both of them work so that they can provide for him and the family better, and that he is old enough to be independent and he can ask for more support from his parents when needed. In essence, CBT helps the client to change his maladaptive cognitive schema, such as overgeneralisation in this case (i.e., the underlying thought pattern that a small number of people is equal to no one) to a realistic, functional analysis of the situation through a reality check.

Such changes in the client's cognitive pattern are expected to make him feel less negatively about the situation, thus enabling him to adopt healthier coping strategies as an alternative to online social relationships. However, it should be noted that desired behavioural changes do not necessarily come about immediately after the changed thoughts and belief systems. Even if the client has corrected his maladaptive cognitions, behavioural changes may take longer to be brought out. Hence, the therapist usually works with the clients to improve behavioural skills as well. These include social skills training, such as time management skills training and interpersonal skills training, to help the client better regulate time spent online, prioritise and carry out daily tasks, and build and maintain supportive relationships with family members and peers.

As mentioned earlier, the strength of CBT is the robust empirical evidence for its effectiveness, relative to other treatment models for Internet and gaming addictions. Indeed, cognitive-behavioural approaches have demonstrated their effectiveness in treating various other impulse control disorders such as pathological gambling, compulsive shopping, bulimia nervosa, and binge eating (Abreu & Góes, 2011). As such, when it comes to treatment of Internet and gaming addictions, which are also considered impulse control disorders, many practitioners have turned to CBT for a treatment model.

Despite its positive result, the limitations of CBT in treating Internet and gaming addictions, especially among the youth, should also be considered. First, CBT tends to overly focus on the individual client as the target of change, neglecting the importance of interactions and interrelationships between individual, family, group and community. Compared with adults, children and adolescents need a greater deal of support and resources from parents, family, friends, teachers, and other adults for their healthy development. Given that their developmental and adjustment outcomes are heavily influenced by their social environments and interactions in general, engaging other people and social systems in the process of treating youth Internet and gaming addictions is critical to full, long-term effects of the intervention. Second, as the therapy intervenes in cognitive structure, process and patterns, a certain degree of the client's intellectual capacity is often a necessary condition for CBT to be effective. For younger children, however, cognitive restructuring may be challenging because their intellectual capacity might not have reached the required level for such a cognitive exercise. Third, CBT may be too structured and directive for some youth. Extroverted or athletic youth or those with short attention spans may be more responsive to an intervention in a flexible format with experiential activities than highly structured and directive interventions like CBT.

FAMILY THERAPY

Family therapy is another psychotherapeutic intervention that is often considered in treatment of Internet and gaming addictions. It involves the whole family rather than only the individual as "the client". It is believed that a dysfunctional family process (e.g., intergenerational family history, family structure, and family communication) underlies the presenting problem of Internet or gaming addiction. For example, parents may have given their child too much power to set rules about his or her daily routines in general or the dysfunctional communication patterns between parents and children are in some way perpetuating a longer-term struggle about Internet use at home. Also, family conflict caused by the child's excessive use of Internet and gaming is another issue itself to be addressed in addition to the primary problem of Internet or gaming addiction. Therefore, a family therapy intervention aims to treat addiction to the Internet or gaming by enhancing family functioning.

Although the importance of working with family is an emerging theme in the area of Internet and gaming addiction treatment, literature that specifically documents suitable family therapy models and the implementation details for treating Internet or gaming addiction is scanty. Keith W Beard's introduction of Multi-Dimensional Family Therapy (MDFT; 2011) is one of the few examples for adolescents addicted to the Internet. In his suggested model, the therapist can work with the adolescent alone, the parent(s) alone and/or have a joint meeting with the adolescent and the parent(s) together. While helping the adolescent with his or her communication skills, coping skills, emotion regulation, problem solving skills, and school performance (the adolescent domain), the family therapist concurrently works with the parents to improve their parenting skills and behavioural and emotional involvement with the adolescent (the parental domain). The therapist also intervenes in the family process by helping the family as a unit of treatment to reduce conflict and increase parent-child emotional attachment within the family system (the interactional domain), extending the intervention to developing family competency in other social systems in which the adolescent is involved, such as in school (the extra-familial domain). The ultimate outcome of alleviation or elimination of Internet or gaming addiction is expected to be achieved by meeting the mediating goal of enhanced family functioning through this holistic intervention in the family system.

Considering its conceptual foundation, family therapy is expected to be a useful treatment approach to Internet and gaming addictions if the family has past or ongoing family issues, such as marital conflict, divorce, or if one or more other family members is struggling with addiction or mental illness. It would also be useful for a youth client from a family experiencing severe role conflict among its members and/or poor family communication. Family therapy can be resource-intensive and time-consuming as it involves not only the individual client but also other family members or the entire family system, if and whenever possible. Thus, the client's and his or her family members' strong commitment to and active engagement in the treatment are critical for successful results. In addition, empirical evidence for the effectiveness of family therapy in the areas of Internet and gaming addictions is yet to be established.

MULTI-DIMENSIONAL COUNSELLING

Multi-dimensional or multi-level counselling is a rather generic terminology referring to an intervention modality recently developed for treating Internet and gaming addictions. This model is not a psychotherapy model and is a main intervention approach employed in Singapore, Hong Kong and South Korea. Unlike CBT and family therapy mentioned previously, which have been originally developed to treat other mental disorders (in the case of CBT) and family malfunctioning (in the case of family therapy), the multi-dimensional counselling program is designed solely for treating Internet and gaming addictions. Basically, a typical multi-dimensional counselling programme for youth with Internet or gaming addiction consists of individual and/or group counselling, peer support or mentoring groups, diversification activities, and psychoeducation along with consultation for parents. A specific example of multi-dimensional counselling for youth Internet or gaming addiction is the local programme run by TOUCH Cyber Wellness (TCW).

TCW's multi-dimensional counselling programme starts with screening and assessment after referral. Youth clients who are referred to TCW will go through the screening process for counsellors to determine whether they are pathological gamers. Out of 10 screening items adapted from the DSM criteria for pathological gambling (now similar to those for Internet Gaming Disorder in DSM-5), the youth is eligible and strongly encouraged to participate in the programme if he or she endorses five or more items. After screening, the counsellor conducts extensive assessment which includes patterns of gaming habits, academic performance, school relationships, parent-child relationships and communication, and the needs of parents in coping with the child's excessive gaming.

In general, the main goals of the counselling are to reduce the symptoms of gaming addiction, to improve school performance (school attendance, homework submission, exam preparation), reduce parent-child conflict caused by gaming addiction and hopefully, improve parent-child relationships. These goals are expected to be met through the following counselling activities:

- Individual/group counselling – Although the counsellor taps on cognitive-behavioural or motivational interviewing techniques where appropriate, individual/

group counselling in this intervention model is mostly psychoeducational in nature. The focus of the initial stage is the youth client's self-awareness. The counsellor starts the intervention process by helping the youth to gain self-awareness in three areas: 1) his or her own gaming behaviours compared with the dangers and symptoms of Internet or gaming addiction in general; 2) his or her academic interests, abilities and future career choice; and 3) his or her behavioural and communication styles at home and their strengths and weaknesses. Once coming to know more about himself or herself and gaining insight into the problem, the youth client is guided with concrete steps to tackle the identified issues through time management and meaningful communication with parents, family members, peers and teachers.

- Peer support group and/or group mentoring – This component is a livelier, group work platform for the youth client to learn more from lived experiences of peers and mentors who used to be addicted to games about how gaming addiction is related to self-identity, academic performance and pursuits, and interpersonal issues. Group members and/or mentors share their own experiences with the group. Also, this group engages in activities together after which they play computer games together for a set time. Some of these activities can include study group, community service (e.g., a home cleaning project for the elderly staying by themselves), motivation talks conducted by TCW staff and watching a movie.

- Outdoor activities – The component of outdoor activities (e.g., football, basketball, kayaking, hiking, and fishing) aims to help the youth client to discover and develop interests in new hobbies or meaningful, healthy leisure activities to prevent overindulgence in gaming. Also, through these activities, the youth is encouraged to apply and reinforce knowledge and skills taught in the counselling and group work sessions in real world situations. The outdoor activities as well as the activities conducted through the peer support mentoring groups form an important element of TCW's multi-dimensional counselling programme known as "Diversification" – where the youth's attention is diverted from pathological gaming and Internet use by exposing them to various alternate real world activities. This diversification approach aims to promote and encourage youths to work towards living a balanced lifestyle.

- Parent consultation – The multi-dimensional counselling programme provides psychoeducation and consultation on the child's gaming addiction for parents. As these parents often feel incompetent in parenting and coping with the child's addiction, this support intervention is centred on effective parenting, gaming and gaming addiction, sharing and consulting on specific challenges identified through the counsellor's work with the youth client, sharing of the youth client's profile (e.g., the youth's self-identified academic interests, abilities and career choice and behavioural and communication patterns) and reflections done during the programme.

Overall, the multi-dimensional counselling programme at TCW is experiential and hands-on. For example, time management skills are not only taught in counselling sessions but practice of these skills is also required of the youth clients in the other programme activities. When youths come to the cyber wellness centre on Saturdays for the peer support mentoring programme, they are instructed to start doing their homework and reading, which is followed by a group session on the topic of the day – e.g., goal setting or sharing by a former game addict. Only after finishing homework and the group session can they play computer games together with other youth clients for a set time. After playing games, they are invited to participate in an outdoor activity.

Superficially, MDFT and multi-dimensional counselling for Internet and gaming addictions may look similar to each other. However, it should be noted there are fundamental differences between the two. As a family therapy model, the focus of MDFT is on the family process, and the therapist does more in-depth clinical work with the family system. In multi-dimensional counselling, the emphasis on the family system is not as strong. Instead, the multi-dimensional counselling programme is designed mainly to cater to the developmental needs of youth, which are centred on self-identity, self-awareness, exposure to a variety of direct and indirect life experiences, and supportive relationships with parents as well as peers and schools.

Unlike CBT and family therapy, which are likely to be accessed at private practice settings, multi-dimensional counselling programmes are much more available and accessible at the community level, and thus less stigmatising. The aforementioned TCW and a few other family service centres in Singapore provide multi-dimensional counselling for youths with Internet or gaming addictions as community-based programmes. In addition, programme activities that are palatable to and practical for youth are another advantage of this intervention model. Such a trait is highly instrumental in engaging youth clients in the treatment process. Another strength of multi-dimensional counselling provided at TCW in particular is that counsellors are gamers themselves. Their savviness in games is of great help in rapport building with youths and makes the youth clients feel well understood. Thus, TCW counsellors make good role models and mentors for their youth clients during the programme.

Although there are many anecdotal success stories about multi-dimensional counselling, empirical evidence for its effectiveness is very rare. Also, since it covers a broad range of issues related to Internet and gaming addictions, as opposed to going into the depths of each issue, it may be less effective for youth who are severely addicted to the Internet or gaming or facing other mental health problems (e.g., ADHD, social anxiety, clinical depression), problematic behaviours (e.g., violent and/or illegal acts) or complicated family issues in addition to Internet or gaming addiction. Also, for the programme to effect the desired changes, the clients' long-term and regular participation in the programme seems to be crucial.

PSYCHIATRIC TREATMENT

As addiction in general is understood as a mental disorder, some people seek psychiatric treatment in the form of a medical intervention for Internet or gaming addiction. Although there are a few experimental studies on pharmacological treatment of Internet and gaming addictions, which were conducted mainly in China and South Korea, empirical research evidence for its effectiveness is still rather unclear, otherwise mixed.

In Singapore, the major provider of psychiatric services for addiction including Internet and gaming addictions is the National Addictions Management Service (NAMS), operated under the Institute of Mental Health (IMH). As Chua (2014) described in his book, the treatment approach of NAMS for Internet and gaming addictions does not aim for total abstinence. Instead, through psychiatric assessment, therapeutic counselling, and medication if necessary, a multi-disciplinary team of psychiatrists, social workers, family therapists, and counsellors works with youth to reduce symptoms and restore healthy psychosocial functioning. Given that treatment is administered in a psychiatric setting, it is believed that psychiatric intervention would be most beneficial for youths with past, current or suspected mental health problems, such as ADHD, social anxiety, depression or autistic spectrum disorder.

BOOT CAMP

Boot camp programmes for Internet and gaming addictions, a cold-turkey method, seem to be a popular treatment model in China and South Korea. Youth sent to a boot camp programme for their Internet or gaming addiction usually stay in a rehabilitation camp facility with no access to digital media and the Internet, under tight surveillance for about a week or two. A boot camp programme usually provides therapy sessions for youth participants, along with a wide range of indoor and outdoor activities including sports, art and/or music classes, and other recreational activities to diversify their interests. Some of such programmes may appear similar to military training.

Except boot camp programme providers' own internal evaluation and anecdotal cases of success portrayed in news media, no scientific empirical research on the effectiveness of the boot camp approach has been conducted. Testimonials from former youth participants in boot camp programmes suggest that the intervention model may have a short-term effect, but its sustainability in the long-run is highly questionable as the treatment is implemented in a highly controlled environment, far from the actual environment in which youths live, with digital media and Internet access. As Beard (2011) rightly pointed out, this type of cold-turkey method does not seem to be realistic. Furthermore, boot camp programmes that allow for camp instructors' physical discipline toward youth participants cause concerns for the participants' safety. To our knowledge, no boot camp programme for Internet or gaming addiction is offered in Singapore.

SUMMARY: HELPFUL COMPONENTS

Even within one intervention modality, actual treatment programmes are varied to a great extent, by adapting from therapeutic elements and operational strategies of the other intervention modalities. With little empirical evidence, it is far from conclusive which intervention model is most effective for treating Internet and gaming addictions as of yet. However, based on available data from researchers' systematic observations and preliminary analyses of existing programmes (e.g., Young, 1999 cited in Abreu, & Góes, 2011) as well as practitioners' and youth clients' feedback, some common features across various intervention programmes seem to make treatment more useful and effective. Thus, the following components can be considered for improving an existing programme or developing a new one. Some of the components have also been mentioned by Young (1999 cited in Abreu, & Góes, 2011).

SUPPORT SERVICES FOR PARENTS OR THE FAMILY

The fact that it is usually parents who first come forward for professional help, rather than the child addicted to the Internet or gaming, implies that the family, especially the parents, needs help as much as the child. Regardless of whether it is family therapy or not, adequate professional support for parents must be in place within the intervention programme. The basic support intervention for parents includes psychoeducation on Internet or gaming addiction. In many cases, parents are quite unfamiliar with online activities and games in which the child engages and do not understand what motivates the child to stay online or play games for a prolonged period. Orienting parents to the child's virtual world and how it develops to addiction is critical in the support intervention for parents. Also, parents need to be equipped with more effective parenting skills and parent-child communication skills. Last but not least, the counselor or therapist's progressive feedback to parents is highly important to inform them on what has been taught to the child during treatment so that it can be practiced and reinforced at home.

TRAINING ON LIFE SKILLS AND COPING STRATEGIES

To overcome behavioural addiction like Internet and gaming addictions, behavioural modification is essential. As such, the importance of managing time and regulating one's own emotions and behaviours has been highlighted repeatedly in the intervention models described above. For an intervention programme to be effective, youth clients need a platform to acquire concrete skills and techniques to address emotional, behavioural and interpersonal patterns related to Internet or gaming addiction.

DIVERSIFICATION ACTIVITIES

Often, youths with Internet or gaming addiction report that they started playing games or surfing the Internet out of boredom, i.e., there is nothing more interesting for them to do. As adopted by many intervention programmes, exposure to a variety of leisure and recreational activities seems to help break overindulgence in one addictive online activity. These activities can also motivate youth to participate and stay on in the programme and help build a peer support system.

COMMUNITY-BASED PROGRAMMES

When a youth suffering from Internet or gaming addiction or his or her parent wants to seek professional help, the first question that they would have is where to go. For many, therapists or psychiatrists in a clinic or hospital setting may not be their most preferred choice of professionals to go to due to their relative inaccessibility and associated stigma. In this regard, community-based programmes would be more accessible for those in need of treatment for Internet or gaming addiction.

USE OF POSITIVE PEER INFLUENCES

Some parents may believe that Internet addiction, particularly addiction to online gaming, is mainly attributed to peer pressure to play games. Although it is not entirely untrue, it has been consistently found in research that low social support is significantly associated with high levels of Internet and gaming addictions (e.g., Wang & Wang, 2013). In other words, people are more likely to become addicted to the virtual world when they feel they are lacking meaningful, supportive social relationships in the real world. As such, feeling understood, accepted and supported from their peers can be highly therapeutic. Thus if a treatment intervention is run in a group format that allows the clients to share one's experiences for empathic understanding and find a mentor or role model who can support their efforts to overcome addition, it can be more beneficial than an intervention that consists only of individual sessions.

RAPPORT WITH THE COUNSELLOR OR THERAPIST

Rapport between practitioner and client, or therapeutic alliance is well known to be one of the most crucial elements of any successful psychosocial intervention. Treatment of Internet and gaming addictions is no exception. Moreover, there seems to be one particular quality of the practitioner that contributes to strong rapport building with youth clients: the practitioner's familiarity with the virtual world. This quality is more critical when the practitioner is working with a youth client with gaming addiction in particular. As shown in TCW's multi-dimensional counselling programme, if the practitioner has some hands-on knowledge about gaming, the youth client would feel better understood, and hence would become more strongly committed to the treatment.

FURTHER DEVELOPMENT OF INTERVENTION PROGRAMMES
RESEARCH

To date, there is little research evidence for the effectiveness of any of the intervention models in treating Internet and gaming addictions, except CBT. However, even the CBT approach examined in prior research takes various forms, combined with certain elements from other intervention models, for example, family-based work or peer support group. Therefore, it is not known which specific components of a treatment programme contribute to its effectiveness. Although some potentially helpful treatment components are described above, scientific evidence that supports the effectiveness of those components are still much needed.

TREATMENT SERVICE DELIVERY SYSTEM

In Singapore, there is no streamlined system for delivering treatment services for youths with Internet and gaming addictions and their families. When a youth or his or her parent decides to seek professional help for the youth's Internet or gaming addiction, they often do not know whom to consult and from where. Although compulsory cyber wellness education programmes (as prevention programmes) are carried out in Singapore secondary schools to inform students of available treatment services, such information often fails to reach their parents and other adult caregivers. However, as in most cases, it is parents, not children, who initiate to seek help from professionals. Thus, it is important to disseminate the information to parents, teachers, and other helping professionals within the community. Another issue in the service delivery system concerns treatment settings. As mentioned earlier, a community-based treatment programme can be more accessible and less stigmatising. However, in reality, the number of community-based programmes is still very limited and many require further development.

Nevertheless, parents or caregivers of individuals who are at risk can obtain help from the following services, with more information found at the back of this book:

NATIONAL ADDICTIONS MANAGEMENT SERVICE (NAMS)

NAMS runs a range of programmes such as:
- National Gambling Helpline: 1800-6-668668 (1800-X-Gamble)

For gambling addiction-related information and appointment making.

- All Addictions helpline: 6-7326837 (6-RECOVER)
  For all other addictions-related information and appointment making.

Web chat services are available via the NAMS website at www.nams.sg

TOUCH CYBER WELLNESS

www.touchcyberwellness.org
TOUCHLine: 1800 377 2252

TOUCHLine is the only cyber wellness helpline in Singapore. A service of TOUCH Community Services, the helpline is manned by a team of counsellors and is in operation weekdays (Mondays to Fridays) from 9am to 6pm. Parents and teachers can contact the helpline if they or their child/student has cyber wellness-related issues to resolve.

For more information and enquiries about cyber wellness and new media literacy programmes for children, youths, parents, educators, professionals and practitioners, please visit www. touchcyberwellness.org or email TOUCH Cyber Wellness at cyberwellness@touch.org.sg

FEI YUE COMMUNITY SERVICES (PROJECT 180)

www.fycs.org

Tel: 6422 1599 ext 599

Project 180 runs a range of services and programmes such as:

- eCounselling Centre (www.egen.sg) – an online facility offering free counselling to youths.
- New Media programme – topics covered include how to protect young users from gaming addiction, blogging, social networking, cybersex and online pornography.

For more information, email project180@fycs.org

CYBERSPORTS AND ONLINE GAMING ASSOCIATION

www.scoga.org

For information on cyber wellness and digital literacy programmes. The association aims to make a difference in the local gaming scene, especially in promoting Cybersports, or more commonly known as eSports.

FUTURE TECHNOLOGY

Dr Huu Kim Le

At the time of publication of this book, the future's Internet technology has already been invented, developed and released. New technologies will always be offered as something that people can gain: enjoyment, enhancement or social status.

We must remember that the latest Internet technology is developed and sold to make money. It is in the Internet companies' interest to keep the user online as often as possible, for as long as possible. Companies will not warn consumers how they do this, how much is too much nor when to stop. Users need to keep this in mind, as each new technology comes with potentially new problems.

When introduced to new technology, users should ask themselves three questions:
• Do I really understand how this technology can help me?
• Can this technology cause me harm?
• Do I really need this technology?

To help answer these questions on the effects of technology, it may be useful to turn to online resources. Guides, reviews and forums available online help inform of the latest technologies. For example, Commonsensemedia.org is a good website that offers independent ratings on different forms of media to assist parents in making smart choices for their families. Other parents offer their opinions on the suitability of different shows, movies and games for children of different ages.

There are also articles and blogs covering a range of topics from digital citizenship to parenting and education. These guides may inform of the benefits and risks of different technologies and media. When asking, "do I really need this technology?" one needs to consider his or her current goals in life. By answering the first two questions adequately, a user will understand how a new technology makes an impact on his or her life goals. The last question is ultimately a choice that a user must make based on this knowledge.

HOW TECHNOLOGY MAY AFFECT BEHAVIOUR IN THE FUTURE
CURRENT TECHNOLOGY ON A LARGER SCALE

In the future, free WiFi and Internet data will be everywhere. How will that affect those individuals, agencies or institutions already grappling with technology problems?

In the future, it may be hard to restrict and protect your child's use of technology unless companies and governments show leadership, set ethical standards and assume responsibility. Many parents feel that they are fighting a losing battle on restricting their child's use of technology. How can you protect your child when they are surrounded by technology in their schools, shopping malls and public spaces? Also, agencies and institutions trying to curb this problem can only do so much to educate and teach others about the dangers of technology. In the end it is the choice of the individual, and a difficult one at that, when there are external influences like advertising and marketing strategies sending the wrong messages to the community.

WEARABLE TECHNOLOGY

This is already available now, from optical head-mounted displays to activity trackers. Humans have always innovated and used technology on our bodies. Clothing that keeps our bodies warm and wristwatches are examples of basic technology commonly used in daily life. But what if these technologies are connected to the Internet? A simple jacket can become "wearable technology". In the popular movie *Back to the Future II*, main character Marty sported "wearable technology" (his shoes and jacket). Science fiction is now a reality. New Internet technology will constantly try to grab our attention, through monitoring us, notifying us and alerting us.

In the future, it will be very difficult to escape from technology. It may be impossible to "unplug" from the Internet as we will live online entirely in an altered state of reality. Privacy of private personal details will also be a problem as we become more connected to the Internet. Companies of these technologies will collect and have ownership of our data. With all this technology monitoring our behaviour this may also cause an undue amount of anxiety and worry.

VIRTUAL REALITY TECHNOLOGY

Virtual reality technology promises to make gaming more immersive, more exciting and for some, potentially more addictive. It will revolutionise how we socialise, communicate and relate to each other. On the other hand, virtual reality technology can be harnessed as a tool to be used for behavioural therapy such as exposing and desensitising an individual who has a phobia to a certain situation, object or creature. The individual can hence experience the full extent of the fear without being actually exposed to the threat itself, and the therapy could be conducted readily and safely in a clinic or laboratory setting.

Virtual reality is an exciting possibility. New virtual worlds or simulations can be artificially designed. New digital environments and undiscovered frontiers are programmable. Consider the science fiction movies *The Matrix* and *Total Recall* as examples. Virtual worlds were designed in these stories to simulate other worlds (the 1990's and Mars respectively). In the future, it may be possible to immigrate to these virtual worlds completely and live there forever. Throughout history, man has immigrated and colonised new worlds in order to find better lives. Virtual worlds may offer an alternative existence. At first, this may seem like a better and safer option for mankind. However, from these movies we have learnt that humans will always question their existence and seek truth and purpose. We will always gravitate towards a preference for reality. This shift will pose difficulties in the future as we will have to physically, emotionally and cognitively rebuild our lives.

In many ways, our current prevention and treatment programmes for those with Internet gaming addiction are already doing this because children are spending a majority of their lives online, missing out on essential life skills. In the movie *The Matrix*, the protagonist Neo questions his mundane life and existence. He seeks truth and eventually decides to leave The Matrix. Because he was born in The Matrix, his whole body must be rebuilt, as he has never used his muscles. He then must be taught about the harsh realities of the real world and how mankind allowed technology made by them to overtake and control their world. Despite this, Neo continues to learn how to fight The Matrix and help others. Meanwhile, Cypher betrays the team so he can leave the real world and return to The Matrix. The moral of the story is that man will continue to innovate and create technology without really considering the implications and consequences. Also, even if the real world becomes unbearable, virtual reality, no matter how well designed, can never fulfill the human need and desire for truth.

eSPORTS

This is already a very popular past time for young people to watch professional gamers compete against each other to determine the most skillful players. One example would be the international Dota 2 championship tournament. These competitions offer lucrative prize money and glamourise Internet gaming. Currently, gaming companies sponsor these competitions as a way to market their games to young people. The evolution of these types of competitions will influence our view of Internet gaming technology.

FUTURE RESEARCH

Much research has been done on the effects of Internet technology on our lives, such as addiction. In the future, researchers will be able to confidently agree, explain and confirm that we can be addicted to Internet technology. This will affect how the government, schools and communities relate to the technology so that we are in control of it and not a slave to our own creations.

In the future, we will be able to understand more about how this technology can change our brain structure and the chemicals in the brain. One good example will be to understand more about the effects of technology on the development of infants and young children, especially the effects on a child's social, emotional and behavioural development.

With time, we will be able to have more tests to determine how these changes have affected our brains, how to find these changes and help us to target new treatments. Already in South Korea, researchers are using brain wave technology to read how the brain is functioning and using brain specific treatments to manage Internet gaming addiction.

Future research will also be able to tell us how individual differences and experiences may shape our relationship to technology. For example, researchers may be able to show the differences between children addicted to Internet gaming from the United States compared to children from Singapore. This will affect how we treat these problems and tailor programmes for the needs of each patient. We will also have more long-term studies on the effect of technology and the effectiveness of different treatments.

Like most new technologies, the invention of the Internet is a double-edged sword. It brings more convenience and enjoyment, and at times furthers knowledge to the people using it, but it can also create new problems such as addictions and other interpersonal, legal and financial complications. Most importantly, our relationship with technology will evolve as the world evolves. It may be possible that future society accepts that people can spend a significant part of their lives online and this is not a disorder but a way of life. It is up to the society and culture to determine how we live with technology around us.

REFERENCES

Activity tracker. (n.d.). In *Wikipedia*. Retrieved from https://en.wikipedia.org/wiki/Activity_tracker

American Psychiatric Association. (2013). *Diagnostic and statistical manual of mental disorders* (5th ed.). Washington, D.C: American Psychiatric Association.

Andrei, L. E., & Paraipan, C. (2015). Internet Addiction Disorder: Current and future perspectives. *Romanian Journal of Child & Adolescent Psychiatry, 3*(1), 28-38.

Beard, K. W. (2011). Working with adolescents addicted to the Internet. In K. S. Young & C. N. de Abreu (Eds.), *Internet Addiction: A Handbook and Guide to Evaluation and Treatment* (pp. 173-189). Hoboken, NJ: John Wiley & Sons.

Bourne, L. (2015, April 7). Inside the Growing Problem of Online Shopping Addiction. Retrieved from http://stylecaster.com/online-shopping-addiction/

Cami, J., & Farre, M. (2003). Drug addiction. *The New England Journal of Medicine, 349,* 975-986.

Central Narcotics Bureau. (2015, July 7). *Drug Situation Report 2014.* Retrieved from http://www.cnb.gov.sg/drugsituationreport/drugsituationreport2014.aspx

Chen, S. H., Weng, L. J., Su, Y. J., Wu, H. M., & Yang, P. F. (2003). Development of a Chinese Internet Addiction Scale and its psychometric study. *Chinese Journal of Psychology, 45*(3), 251-266.

Choo, H. (2012). *Profiles of pathological gamers and their families.* Paper presented at the Serious Gaming & Social Connect, 4-6 October 2012, Singapore.

Choo, H., Gentile, D. A., Sim, T., Li, D., Khoo, A., & Liu, A. (2010). Pathological video-gaming among Singaporean youth. *Annals Academy Of Medicine Singapore, 39*(11), 822-829.

Choo, H., Sim, T., Liau, A. K. F., Gentile, D. A., & Khoo, A. (2015). Parental influences on pathological symptoms of video-gaming among children and adolescents: A prospective study. *Journal of Child and Family Studies, 24*(5), 1429-1441.

Chua, R. S. B. (2014). *Virtual realms, real needs: How to guide your children in a world of videogames.* Singapore: Armour.

Computer Misuse Act, Cap 50A, Rev. Ed. 2007, Singapore.

Crosson-Tower, C. (2005). *Understanding child abuse and neglect* (6th ed.). Boston: Allyn & Bacon.

Davis, R. A. (2001). A cognitive-behavioral model of pathological Internet use. *Computers in Human Behavior, 17*(2), 187-195.

de Abreu, C. N., & Góes, D. S. (2011). Psychotherapy for Internet addiction. In K. S. Young & C. N. de Abreu (Eds.), *Internet Addiction: A Handbook and Guide to Evaluation and Treatment* (pp. 155-171). Hoboken, NJ: John Wiley & Sons.

Edwards, G., & Gross, M. M. (1976) Alcohol dependence: Provisional description of a clinical syndrome. *British Medical Journal, 1*(6017), 1058-1061.

Greenfield, D. (2011). The addictive properties of Internet usage. In K. S. Young & C. N. de Abreu (Eds.), *Internet Addiction: A Handbook and Guide to Evaluation and Treatment* (pp. 135-153). Hoboken, NJ: John Wiley & Sons.

Griffiths, M. (2001). Sex on the Internet: Observations and implications for Internet sex addiction. *The Journal of Sex Research, 38*(4), 333-342.

Grohol, J. M. (2012, October 26). *Internet Addiction Guide.* Retrieved from http://psychcentral.com/netaddiction/

Ha, J. H., Yoo, H. J., Cho, I. H., Chin, B., Shin, D., & Kim, J. H. (2006). Psychiatric comorbidity assessed in Korean children and adolescents who screen positive for Internet addiction. *Journal of Clinical Psychiatry, 67*(5), 821-826.

Ho, R. C., Zhang, M. W., Tsang, T. Y., Toh, A. H., Pan, F., Lu, Y., Cheng, C., Yip, P. S., Lam, L. T., Lai, C. M., Watanabe, H., & Mak, K. K. (2014). The association between Internet addiction and psychiatric co-morbidity: A meta-analysis. *BMC Psychiatry, 14*, 183.

Infocomm Development Authority of Singapore. (2014). *Annual Survey on Infocomm Usage in Households and by Individuals for 2013.* Retrieved from https://www.ida.gov.sg/~/media/Files/Infocomm%20Landscape/Facts%20and%20Figures/SurveyReport/2013/2013HHmgt.pdf

Khoo, A., & Hall, M. J. (2010). *Welcome to our world: Connecting parents with gamers.* Singapore: McGraw-Hill Education.

King, D. L., Delfabbro, P. H., Zwaana, T., & Kaptsis, D. (2013). Clinical features and Axis 1 comorbidity of Australian adolescent pathological Internet and video game users. *Australian and New Zealand Journal of Psychiatry, 47*(11), 1058-1067

Ko, C. H., Yen, J. Y., Yen, C. F., Chen, C. S., & Chen, C. C. (2012). The association between Internet addiction and psychiatric disorder: A review of the literature. *European Psychiatry, 27*(1), 1-8.

Kuss, D. J., & Griffiths, M. D. (2012). Online gaming addiction in children and adolescents: A review of empirical research. *Journal of Behavioral Addictions, 1*(1), 3-22.

Kuss, D. J., Griffiths, M. D., Karila, L., & Billieux, J. (2014). Internet addiction: A systematic review of epidemiological research for the last decade. *Current Pharmaceutical Design, 20*(25), 1-26.

Laier, C., Pawlikowski, M., Pekal, J., Schulte, F. P., & Brand, M. (2013). Cybersex addiction: Experienced sexual arousal when watching pornography and not real-life sexual contacts makes the difference. *Journal of Behavioral Addictions, 2*(2), 100–107.

Lee, J., Hwang, J. Y., Park, S. M., Jung, H. Y., Choi, S. W., Lee, J. Y., & Choi, J. S. (2014). Differential resting-state EEG patterns associated with comorbid depression in Internet addiction. *Progress in Neuro-Psychopharmacology and Biological Psychiatry, 50*, 21-26.

Ma, H. K. (2011). Internet addiction and antisocial Internet behavior of adolescents. *The Scientific World Journal, 11*, 2187-2196.

Meerkerk, G. J., Van Den Eijnden, R. J., Vermulst, A. A., & Garretsen, H. F. (2009) The Compulsive Internet Use Scale (CIUS): Some psychometric properties. *Cyberpsychology & Behaviour, 12*(1), 1-6.

Mythily, S., Qiu, S., & Winslow, M. (2008). Prevalence and correlates of excessive Internet use among youth in Singapore. *Annals Academy Of Medicine Singapore, 37*(1), 9-14.

Nielson Company. (2012, February 23). *State of the Media: U.S. Digital Consumer Report, Q3-Q4 2011.* Retrieved from http://www.nielsen.com/us/en/insights/reports/2012/us-digital-consumer-report.html

Optical head-mounted display. (n.d.). In *Wikipedia.* Retrieved from https://en.wikipedia.org/wiki/Optical_head-mounted_display

Shaw, M., & Black, D. W. (2008). Internet addiction: Definition, assessment, epidemiology and clinical management. *CNS Drugs, 22*(5), 353-365.

Sim, K., Sengupta, S., Fung, D. S. S., & Chee, K. T. (Eds.). (2014). *Essential guide to psychiatry.* Singapore: Pearson Education South Asia.

S'pore youths spending more time online: Study. (2013, January 11). *Yahoo! Newsroom.* Retrieved from https://sg.news.yahoo.com/s-pore-youths-spending-more-time-online--study-100333925.html

Twohig, M. P., & Crosby, J. M. (2010). Acceptance and commitment therapy as a treatment for problematic Internet pornography viewing. *Behavior Therapy, 41*(3), 285-295.

University of Maryland Medical Center. (2014, March 10). *Pathological Gambling.* Retrieved from https://umm.edu/health/medical/ency/articles/pathological-gambling

Urbas, G. (2008). An overview of cybercrime legislation and cases in Singapore. *Asian Law Institute Working Paper Series, No. 001.* Retrieved from https://law.nus.edu.sg/asli/pdf/WPS001.pdf

Wang, E. S. T., & Wang, M. C. H. (2013). Social support and social interaction ties on Internet addiction: Integrating online and offline context. *Cyberpsychology, Behavior, and Social Networking, 16*(11), 843-849.

Widyanto, L., & Griffiths, M. (2006). 'Internet Addiction': A critical review. *International Journal of Mental Health and Addiction, 4*(1), 31-51.

Yalom, I. D., & Leszcz, M. (2005). *The theory and practice of group psychotherapy* (5th ed.). New York: Basic Books.

Young, K. S. (1998). *Caught in the net: How to recognize the signs of Internet addiction and a winning strategy for recovery.* New York: Wiley.

Young, K. S. (2001). *Tangled in the web: Understanding cybersex from fantasy to addiction.* Bloomington, ID: 1st Books Library.

Young, K. S., & de Abreu, C. N. (Eds). (2010). *Internet addiction: A handbook and guide to evaluation and treatment.* Hoboken, NJ: John Wiley & Sons.

Youths won't post false or inaccurate information online: Singapore Poly survey. (2015, January 13). *The Straits Times.* Retrieved from http://www.straitstimes.com/singapore/youths-wont-post-false-or-inaccurate-information-online-singapore-poly-survey

ADDICTIONS-RELATED AND CYBER WELLNESS HELP

For addictions-related and cyber wellness help and intervention outside of Singapore, contact your local addictions management specialist or professional treatment provider.

National Addictions Management Service (NAMS)

www.nams.sg

For general addictions-related information and appointment making, dial the Addictions helpline at:
6-7326837 (6-RECOVER).

For gambling addiction-related information and appointment making, dial the National Gambling helpline at:
1800-6-668668 (1800-X-Gamble).

The National Addictions Management Service was set up in the Institute of Mental Health in 2008 with the support of the Ministry of Health to provide treatment for people with addictions.

NAMS treats patients who are addicted to drugs, alcohol, gambling, the Internet and others. It runs a dedicated outpatient clinic for three different groups of patients – adolescents, private and subsidised patients.

NAMS also has an inpatient ward called Serenity Centre which is a residential facility for patients who require detoxification and rehabilitation. In addition, NAMS runs two satellite clinics at the Institute of Mental Health's Community Wellness Clinics (CWCs) in Queenstown and Geylang.

Its services include:

- Assessment and treatment of addictions by a multi-disciplinary team of psychiatrists, counsellors, psychologists, nurses and medical social workers
- Individual, group and family therapy
- Addiction awareness talks for the community
- Training for healthcare and social service professionals
- Research on addictions

Web chat services are available via the NAMS website at www.nams.sg.

Additional cyber wellness help is also available at:

TOUCH Cyber Wellness (a service of TOUCH Community Services)

www.touchcyberwellness.org

TOUCHLine: 1800 377 2252

TOUCHLine is the only cyber wellness helpline in Singapore. It is manned by a team of counsellors and is in operation weekdays (Mondays to Fridays) from 9am to 6pm. Parents and teachers can contact the helpline if they or their child/ student has cyber wellness-related issues to resolve. For more information and enquiries about cyber wellness and new media literacy programmes for children, youths, parents, educators, professionals and practitioners, email TOUCH Cyber Wellness at cyberwellness@touch.org.sg.

Fei Yue Community Services (Project 180)

www.fycs.org
Tel: 6422 1599 ext 599

Project 180 (Youth Services) is a youth centre under the umbrella of Fei Yue Community Services, established with the support of South East Community Development Council and the National Youth Council (NYC) in 2003. The name "Project 180" represents its mission of life transformation, in the hope that youths and families will be able to experience a 180-degree change in their lives.

The team comprises trained social workers, counsellors and youth workers to provide professional help to youths and families through a variety of programmes and activities.

Project 180 runs a range of services and programmes such as eCounselling Centre (www.egen.sg) – an online facility offering free counselling to youths – and the New Media programme, which touches on topics including how to protect young users from gaming addiction, blogging, social networking, cybersex and online pornography. For more information, email Project 180 at project180@fycs.org.

Cybersports and Online Gaming Association

www.scoga.org

The association runs cyber wellness and digital literacy programmes. The association aims to make a difference in the local gaming scene, especially in promoting Cybersports, or more commonly known as eSports.

CONTRIBUTORS

Ong Say How *MBBS, MMed (Psychiatry), GDip(Psychotherapy)*
Department of Child and Adolescent Psychiatry, Institute of Mental Health

Dr Ong is a senior consultant child psychiatrist and chief in the department of Child & Adolescent Psychiatry, Institute of Mental Health (IMH). He has been deeply engaged in outpatient services for children and adolescents with psychological problems and has conducted research work in mood disorders, schizophrenia and ADHD. Besides being a volunteer as a board member of the Singapore Association for Mental Health (SAMH) and a teaching faculty of undergraduate and postgraduate medical education, Dr Ong is also a frequent speaker in public forums and media interviews on child mental health issues. His authorship also spans various relevant topics on children and adolescent mental health.

Gomathinayagam Kandasami *MBBS., MRCPsych., DPM.*
Chief of Addiction Medicine Department, Institute of Mental Health
Adjunct Assistant professor of psychiatry at Duke Graduate School of Medicine
Adjunct Assistant Professor of psychiatry at NUS YLL School of Medicine

Dr Kandasami is an Addictions Specialist who currently works at National Addictions Management Service (NAMS) in Institute of Mental Health (IMH). He has been actively involved in clinical, training and research activities at NAMS and also holds other administrative roles in IMH. He holds an academic appointment with NUS YLL School of Medicine and Duke NUS Graduate School of Medicine. He has been a Core faculty for the National Psychiatric Residency Program for psychiatry and also teaches at the Graduate Diploma in Mental Health Program for General Practitioners jointly organised by IMH and NUS.

Mythily Subramaniam *MBBS, MD*
Research Division, IMH

Dr Mythily Subramaniam graduated from Lady Hardinge Medical College, India. She is currently the Director of the Research Division and Lead Investigator of the Programme of Mental Health Policy Studies at the Institute of Mental Health. She also has a concurrent teaching appointment at the Saw Swee Hock School of Public Health, National University Singapore. Her main academic and research interests include psychiatric epidemiology, psychosis and addictions. She has published widely in the field of behaviour addictions and is on the editorial board of Addictive Behaviors Reports.

Tan Yi Ren *BA*
Department of Child and Adolescent Psychiatry, Institute of Mental Health

Mr Tan graduated from the Nanyang Technological University with a Bachelor's Degree in Psychology. Since his undergraduate years, he has been particularly interested in the field of child and adolescent psychiatry. He enjoys interacting with children and feels that there is much more work needed to be done in these areas. Currently working as a researcher at IMH's Child Guidance Clinic, Yi Ren conducts and assists with various research projects in Internet addiction, cyberbullying, selective mutism, Attention Deficit Hyperactivity Disorder (ADHD), oppositional defiant disorder and conduct disorder.

Jayanthi d/o Manohar *BA*
National Addictions Management Service, Institute of Mental Health

Ms Jayanthi d/o Manohar, BA Psychology (NUS), is a senior counsellor at the National Addictions Management Service of the Institute of Mental Health with a certification in substance abuse counselling (CSAC) and gambling addiction counselling (CGAC). She has been working in the field of addiction counselling since 2010 providing individual and group counselling and also conducting trainings and workshops. Jayanthi is also leading the adolescent team called ReLive, managing adolescents both for substance and behavioural problems.

Ray Chua Swee Boon *B(Acc), B(Psych), M(Clin.Psych)*
National University Hospital

Ray Chua is a clinical psychologist practising in the National University Hospital. He is a member of the Resource and Early Assessment and Intervention for Community Mental Health (REACH) Service and leads the Cyber Health and Internet Programme. He is the author of *Virtual Realms Real Needs: Guiding your children in a world of videogames.* His previous work experiences include positions at TOUCH Cyber Wellness, ITE (College East) and PSA Corporation.

Huu Kim Le *MBBS, FRANZCP, Cert. Child Adol. Psych*
NSW Institute of Psychiatry

Dr Huu Kim Le is an Australian Child and Adolescent Psychiatrist. He is a board member of the Network for Internet Investigation and Research Australia. In 2015, he conducted an investigation at the Institute of Mental Health in Singapore on Internet gaming. He also collaborated with Internet Gaming Addiction clinics in India and South Korea. Dr Le founded cgiclinic.com, a website to increase Internet gaming and health awareness. He has also given a TEDx Talk titled "The Spell of Immersion" to educate the community about Internet gaming worlds, which is available online.

Melvyn Zhang Weibin *MBBS (Singapore), DCP (RCP&S, Ireland), MRCPsych (UK)*
National HealthCare Group Specialist Registrar / Senior Resident

Dr Melvyn Zhang is currently a senior resident (Year5) in psychiatry with the National Healthcare Group. He has a special interest in addictions and E-health. He helps to run the adolescent clinics in the National Addictions Management Service, and sees youths with Internet and Gaming issues. To date, he has 33 publications, with major publications in the British Medical Journal, Lancet Psychiatry as well as the Journal of Internet Medical Research (JIMR).

Lawrence Tan Kok Kah *BSc (Hons), MA, CSAC, CGAC, CCS*
National Addictions Management Service, Institute of Mental Health

Lawrence Tan, MA Psychology (NTU), (CCS, CSAC, CGAC) is currently working as a Senior Psychologist with the National Addictions Management Service/ Institute of Mental Health. He is the clinical lead for the department's gambling treatment services and oversees the work of therapists working within this realm. Having worked with the department for the past 10 years, Lawrence specialises in the treatment of patients with both substance (drugs and alcohol) and process/behavioural (gambling, cybergaming, compulsive sexual behaviours) addictions.

Jaydip Sarkar MBBS, DPM, DFMH, CCST, CTP, MRCPsych
General & Forensic Psychiatry, Institute of Mental Health

Dr Sarkar is a Consultant Forensic Psychiatrist, who works with mentally disordered offenders in prisons, secure hospital wards, and community. He provides expert opinion to courts and other legal bodies. He has clinical and research interests in patients with severe childhood abuse, adult trauma, severe mental illnesses and personality disorders who present deviant, violent and suicidal behaviours. He also provides psychotherapy and has published many peer-reviewed articles, book chapters and is the author and co-editor of an award-winning book entitled *Clinical Topics in Personality Disorder*.

Hyekyung Choo MSW (Master of Social Work), PhD, Associate Professor
Department of Social Work, National University of Singapore

Hyekyung Choo has been conducting extensive research on health risk behaviours and cyber wellness issues, focusing on gaming disorder, among Singaporean youth in the past ten years. As a social work researcher, she has also been leading and guiding various social service evaluation projects through her teaching and research support for social service providers. With a strong belief in the constructive synergy from inter-professional collaboration, she strives to contribute practical, applied research knowledge to the field.

Chong Ee Jay MA
Manager, TOUCH Cyber Wellness

Chong Ee Jay is a member on board the Media Literacy Council to promote an astute and responsible participatory culture. He is also the Manager of TOUCH Cyber Wellness, a service of TOUCH Community Service. Ee Jay champions public education programmes both locally (through schools, communities and national level efforts) and internationally, as well as counselling intervention and youth mentoring works.